FORGOTTEN DYNAMITE

Forgotten Dynamite

MICHAEL GREEN

KINGSWAY PUBLICATIONS
EASTBOURNE

ISBN 1 84291 120 1

Published by
KINGSWAY COMMUNICATIONS LTD
Lottbridge Drove, Eastbourne BN23 6NT, England.
Email: books@kingsway.co.uk

Book design and production for the publishers by
Bookprint Creative Services, P.O. Box 827, BN21 3YJ, England.
Printed in Great Britain.

For Jane Holloway
Prayer and Evangelism Secretary of the Evangelical Alliance
who for many years worked with me
in preparing and carrying out
evangelistic missions in
the UK and abroad

Contents

A Word from the Author . . .

You may think this is a strange book to write, concentrating as it does on one narrow sphere of evangelism, that of the parish or university mission. Strange it may be, but it is needed all the same. In today's church broadly welcoming noises are often made about evangelism, but not a lot is done. If anything is done, it will probably be one of the 'process' courses introducing people to Christianity, of which the most famous is Alpha: but there are others, such as Credo, Emmaus and Christianity Explained. These are immensely important, not least because they take a good many weeks painstakingly to explain the heart of the gospel to people who are generally virtual strangers to it.

Where, in the homes, the media, the schools or the workplaces of our land, do people get to hear the gospel which formed our culture? Millions of people in Britain are profoundly ignorant of even what gave rise to Christmas, Good Friday and Easter. So of course it is vital to have these process courses, in order to help enquirers understand what Christianity is, and in due course to make an informed decision whether or not to embrace it.

But that is not the only way of evangelism! There are many ways; one of the most neglected these days is the intentional extended mission in a town or university conducted by a team with an experienced leader. I first discovered this form of outreach when I was an undergraduate at Oxford, and I could see that it had limited but real success. Subsequent missions impressed me more. I began first to go on them and then to lead them in universities, including both Oxford and Cambridge, together with towns and whole cities in many countries. I still find it a very effective form not only of bringing new people to faith in Christ, but of mobilising participating local churches and student bodies for the outreach ministry which is their Christian calling.

However, I see few such teams operating these days. I have the privilege of organising several evangelistic missions each year from Wycliffe Hall, which is part of the University of Oxford and specialises in training men and women for the ordained ministry. I want our students to experience the challenge of forming part of a team bringing the gospel in an appropriate way to strangers they have never met and in churches they have never previously visited. But I long to see far more of such missions in the West. In Africa they are common. The fast-growing Anglican dioceses in Tanzania rely heavily on mission teams going out to spread the gospel in the surrounding countryside. Most of the new dioceses in the country have been formed in this way.

And so I want to commend it afresh. It demands knowledge and experience, it requires a high degree of motivation and team spirit, and it calls for courage to come out of the comfort zone and find ways of commending the gospel to a jaded postmodern generation who are suspicious of any absolute truth claims and have to be met on grounds they will accept. It is challenging. It is joyful. And it is one way of obeying the last command of Jesus Christ.

I have made a good deal of use of my own experience in this book, but, as I have been writing on evangelism over many years, I have inevitably drawn to some extent from previous work, particularly *Evangelism through the Local Church,* which circulated widely a decade ago but is now no longer in print. I hope that the Lord whom I serve will be able to use this small work to encourage others either to invite or to take part in evangelistic missions, large or small, at home or abroad. They are forgotten dynamite.

The Context

1

The Evangelistic Mission – What are we talking about?

International companies have 'missions' these days. The military have 'missions'. But what do Christians mean when they talk about 'missions'?

Well, they mean different things, as I discovered when I went to work in Canada. Invited to lead a 'mission' in an Anglican parish in western Canada, I was in for a shock. I expected that the parish would be organised for evangelism in some shape or form: there would be church people keen to invite their unchurched friends to hear the gospel. Not a bit of it. They wanted me to give three addresses on a totally different topic, for which they were prepared to give a hefty honorarium. That was not my idea of a mission. I declined!

In the nineteenth century, a great many churches had 'missions', whether they were Anglo-Catholic or Evangelical in their tradition. It generally meant a clergyman coming from outside the parish and preaching night after night in the local church to the long-suffering parishioners and those they enticed in to listen. That was one understanding of a 'mission'.

Another is much more familiar, although it is generally

called a crusade. It became fashionable when Billy Graham first came to England and led the celebrated Harringay Crusade. The idea was somewhat similar to the nineteenth-century model, though on a much larger scale and much better organised. A visiting preacher, a massive venue, a large number of churches working together, lively singing, testimony from well-known converts, and preaching. But Billy Graham did not leave it at that. He would finish his evangelistic address with the famous words 'I want you to get up out of your seat . . .'. From all over the arena men and women would rise, drawn by a power they did not understand but knew to be important, and stream to the front, standing in front of the evangelist. He prayed for them, and then each of them was passed to a 'counsellor' who gave them a short enquiry about their spiritual state, an evangelistic booklet, a Gospel, and a church to contact for growing in the Christian life. One hopes that those who came forward had come to faith through the preaching, because the counsellors were usually less than highly trained. The counselling procedure was a blunt instrument, in all conscience, but it helped thousands to start genuine Christian discipleship.

Though initially scorned by the church hierarchy, Graham's crusades became so successful that before long almost every bishop was anxious to be seen on the platform supporting him. And crusade evangelism became the premier form of leading a mission. You needed the co-operation of churches, the training of counsellors, the event itself, and the transfer of those who came forward to some church where, hopefully, they would receive nurture. As time went on, the procedure was refined. Proper training courses for new believers were invented and the fall-out became somewhat less. Crusade evangelism was seen to be the appropriate and reasonably effective method for a twentieth-century mission. And despite the fact that nobody else even began to have the impact of Billy Graham himself, this form of evangelism became the model which lesser evangelists strove to follow. So much so that when I went to speak evangelistically for a church their best lay people would generally not invite any of their friends to the event: they would be waiting as counsellors for me to deliver custom into their hands!

But by the eighties, and much sooner in some places, disenchantment began to set in. Not with Billy Graham himself, who retained universal respect, and people on the fringe of the church and beyond would still go to crusades that he ran. But other evangelists did not begin to have the same appeal. Some of them were disgraced by sexual immorality or financial irregularity. And the populace at large began to learn the form. They knew that if you went to one of these events you would be invited out to the front, and it would be embarrassing, and perhaps worse. They were less than enthusiastic at emulating ducks flying over a pond that was ringed with wildfowlers! They determined not to go.

Moreover in the last quarter of the twentieth century a scepticism settled upon much of the Western world. The certainties of the Age of Reason collapsed. No longer could one be sure of a society guided by reason, of the validity of truth, of objective moral standards, of the credibility of politicians and clergy. People became less and less willing to take anything on someone else's say-so. And as a result the crusade model of mission became less and less attractive, at least in Britain, though it retained some of its old power and attractiveness in the United States, especially when led by Billy Graham himself.

When I talk about 'a mission' I do not mean a crusade like that, for all its proven values half a century ago. Nor do I mean a modified version of the nineteenth-century 'mission', with the solo visiting preacher coming in, armed with a prefabricated plan of campaign to be imposed on the recipients. It would be strong on preaching, either in church or wherever else the parish could gather a fair number of people. The one-man band is usually no more effective these days in evangelism than he is as the minister of a church. Partnership, joint leadership, shared initiatives are in. Solo operators are out. We need a team – as we shall see.

In any case, should not mission be the regular work of the church rather than an occasional invasion? What do we mean, then, by talking about 'a mission'?

Let me tell you how I understand it. For many centuries in the Christian church there has been talk of the *missio Dei*, God's mission. By this phrase people have drawn attention to the important truth that mission is God's work. He is our Creator and Redeemer, and mission is supremely his initiative to draw back his rebel subjects into his loving embrace. It is not a human enterprise, for which we may ask God's help. It lies within the very nature of God himself. 'For God [the Father] so loved the world that he gave his only Son that whosoever believes in him should not perish but have everlasting life.' And God the Son not only engaged in calling men and women to repent and commit themselves to him, but died to make possible the reconciliation of sinful human beings with a holy God. And the function of God the Holy Spirit is primarily to continue this divine mission among human beings. Sometimes he does it with sovereign independence: stories abound of people becoming Christians as a result of dreams, visions, healings, exorcisms or reading the Bible. It is supremely God's work. It is the *missio Dei*, his sovereign and loving outreach to his rebellious subjects.

But God is very generous. He often allows human beings to take part in this rescue operation. He will only use those who have themselves been to the cross for forgiveness, and entrusted their lives to the Redeemer. But use them he does. Their lifestyle, their testimony, their acts of loving service, their friendship, their preaching are all channels through which the divine mission can flow. It is the supreme privilege of the church to become partners, co-operators with God. And yet it is always his work. We cannot convince anyone of their need. We cannot make Jesus attractive to anyone. We cannot draw anyone to that humbling place of repentance and faith. We cannot bring about new birth, an entirely new orientation of life towards God and no longer towards self. That is God's work, but often he allows us to share in it.

Very well. That is well known among Christians, if less frequently acted on. It is, after all, the function of the kingdom of God which Jesus was constantly proclaiming. He called people to him so that they would make God King in their lives, offer him the number one spot in every aspect of life, and as a result become the sort of people he could use. Accordingly church is intended not to be a building we enter once a week, but a community of people bonded by love, trust and obedience to their Redeemer. And so the gospel is meant to spread by osmosis. People will be drawn in to this joyful community and want to become part of it.

However, if that is the idea, we have to admit that it only rarely happens. Church is all too often the building people enter from time to time. Increasingly they do not enter it at all. And on the whole those who do are not notable for their joy in being redeemed at great cost by the Lord himself. They do not always demonstrate his love flowing through their lives. They are not universally famous for their care for the lonely and underprivileged. They rarely have the name of Jesus on their lips except, alas, as a swear word. They may be exhorted to reach out to their neighbours with the gospel if they have an enthusiastic vicar, but they do not do it.

Some of them have become so caught up in church culture that they have very few friends outside church circles. Most of them have no idea what it would mean to spread the gospel among their friends. Those who have some idea may feel guilty at not doing it. But they have a lurking suspicion that if they did make a serious attempt to involve their friends and neighbours in church, those friends would either not come or would come and be bored out of their minds. Because, let's face it, most churches and their activities are excruciatingly boring! It seems to be one of the major achievements of the Western church that we have made Jesus, the most exciting person the world has ever seen, boring! So mission, seen as 'in-drag' rather than 'out-reach' is remarkably ineffectual.

This is not just my opinion. The statistics demonstrate it. During the whole of the last hundred years in almost all of Western Europe, Australia, New Zealand and much of North America, church attendance has been dropping in every denomination. It is estimated that during the Decade of Evangelism (AD 1990–2000) the churches in the West lost over a million people. Church attendance in England fell by 20 per cent between 1987 and 1999. More than a thousand young people leave our churches in Britain every week. That shows that 'mission' is either not one of the priorities of the churches, or if it is, it is extraordinarily incompetently executed.

If that is undeniable, then what is the point of a visiting team coming in to facilitate mission? And what would it look like? Those are the questions to which we pay attention in this book. But first we need to glance at the 'postmodern' cultural climate in which we find ourselves. For if we cannot speak to the climate around us, we are doomed to irrelevance.

2

*The Evangelistic Mission –
Who are we talking to?*

It would be hard to exaggerate the change in the spiritual climate in the past 40 years. When the cultural revolution of the sixties burst upon us, the prevailing outlook was that of modernism, as it had been for the previous two centuries. Our educational system was heavily influenced by the eighteenth-century Enlightenment, which largely dispensed with the notion of God, and replaced him with belief in human reason. We, not God, call the shots: he can safely be left in limbo like a constitutional monarch if, indeed, he exists at all. Science, and its resultant technology, would be the key to the future. Belief in progress was widespread: we are moving towards a better future all the time. An increasingly important point was belief in facts: only what can be seen, measured or otherwise empirically verified is real. Everything else, including values and religion, are subjective. They are private matters, and are generally banished from the public square. There was a strong belief in freedom: freedom from tyranny, of course, but also freedom from church, dogma and empire. And finally there was an unspoken assumption about human nature: we all have hearts of gold.

Such were the convictions of the Age of Reason into which everyone currently of middle age and above was born. Such were the assumptions of the culture. Christians, of course, knew that they could not demonstrate the existence of God, the deity of Jesus, the atoning nature of the cross, the reality of the bodily resurrection, and the final divide between heaven and hell. But they spent much energy in showing the reasonableness of these beliefs, and spared no pains seeking out evidence from whatever quarter to back up these convictions. They realised that a great many people believed in God in a vague way, and the function of an 'evangelistic mission' in these circumstances was to build on that vague assumption, turn it into active belief, and precipitate decision for Christ that would lead people into the life of the local church or student body. For all the scepticism of the Enlightenment, many people broadly assented to the Christian claims about God and Jesus, but had never done anything about them. The evangelist's job was to electrify the fence on which they sat.

But in the last four decades a very different social picture has emerged, and a very different strategy is required of the church if it is to gain a hearing. Modernist assumptions about life are no longer convincing. It is apparent that people do not primarily act on the ground of reason alone: think of falling in love, or going to war. Indeed the supremacy of reason has been effectively undermined by three of the great thinkers of the nineteenth century, and the results have only comparatively recently been widely appreciated. Darwin's account of the past, Marx's account of the future, and Freud's account of the psyche leave little room for rationality as the governing factor in human affairs! The 'Modern' worldview was ludicrously optimistic. We are clearly living in a time of massive cultural change, and it is hardly a change for the better. We are destroying the environment – the ozone layer, the rainforests, the land itself – and we are poisoning the seas. We possess the capacity to destroy the world many times over through the stockpiling of nuclear devices, spread over a wide variety of countries and regimes. Forty million (and rising) people across the world are plagued by HIV/AIDS, the most virulent scourge since the Black Death. We are witnessing the breakdown of marriage and the family, the creation of multi-millions of homeless refugees, violence constantly increasing on our streets, a selfish hedonism dominating our lifestyle, and the appalling and growing divide between the rich North and the poverty-stricken South in the world. The problems we face are beyond human control. The myths of the essential goodness of human nature and the inevitability of human progress have worn very thin, not least in the light of two horrific world wars and the Holocaust.

Accordingly, the whole intellectual and cultural package derived from the Enlightenment has become very suspect. The crisis in the Modern worldview has induced a strong reaction which we call Postmodernism (for want of a better name). As with liberalism and colonialism, so it is with Modernity. We are 'post' all that. We are not quite sure what we are, but we know that we have left behind the accumulated worldview of the past two-and-a-half centuries. We are 'after' all that. It has passed its shelf life.

And so these days, after the perceived demise both of Christendom and of the Enlightenment, we find a great suspicion of all 'meta-stories', all attempts to erect over our fragmented experiences an umbrella which can make sense of them. There is no big account of the world left for us to believe, so we are told: only a mosaic of little stories, yours and mine included. In the absence of any widely accepted framework, we must all make our own choices. Choice is the key to it all, whether in the super-market of food or ideas.

And so we find ourselves in a highly relativising climate which, so the academics tell us, denies all absolutes (despite the logical fallacy of making such a claim – to assert that there are no absolutes seems a rather absolute statement to me!). I am not so sure that all absolutes have evaporated. Think of the universal horror of paedophilia. Think of the worldwide revulsion after September 11. It seems that we have some absolutes left. At all events, ours is an age which distrusts all authority figures and structures: Nietzsche's postulate of a naked 'will to power' has come of age with Nazism, Communism, totalitarianism and the multinationals.

There is deep cynicism abroad about big institutions: the legal system, the monarchy, the police, the educa-tional system, the church, parliament, and industry are all viewed with distrust. Morality has no norms. Make up your own idea of what is right for you, but don't try to push it down my throat! And don't talk to me about truth: there is no such thing. You are only trying to force your ideas on others when you speak about truth.

Scorn for the past is matched by loss of hope for the future. The cry is for 'instant' everything. Live for now. Live for self. It is a one-dimensional life. This should not surprise us. If the past is discounted and the future is bleak, all we are left with is the present. If other people do not matter much, you had better take care of yourself: nobody else will.

Needless to say it is an age of visual rather than writ-ten communication, a culture of the worldwide web, not of books. Information is communicated in soundbites and slogans, and TV commercials. Consistency is at a discount, as is logical or linear thinking. Even the law of non-contradiction is rejected by some: they seem to hold several contradictory notions at the same time! An author is not allowed to have a purpose for his book any more. The feminist, the revolutionary, the existentialist will all read their (equally valid – and mutually contradictory) interpretations into the text! All is deconstructed! Subjectivism rules, OK.

It goes without saying, therefore, that in the past 30 years or so, while these massive cultural changes have been taking place, evangelism has necessarily become somewhat different. In some ways it has become easier, in many ways more difficult. No longer do Christian apologists have to be preoccupied with the issues which were so challenging in the Modern age, such as evidence for the existence of God, the possibility of miracle, or the truth of the resurrection. The goalposts of debate have shifted wildly, and Christians have to try to build a house of faith where all foundations are treated as suspect. Facing hearers who may accept no objective truths, no moral norms, no rational arguments, no belief in revelation, they have to attempt to swim against this tide of subjectivism. It is not an easy task either for the local church or student body, or for the evangelist who tries to conduct a 'mission'.

There are other complications which used not to bother us. Forty years ago, Britain was certainly not the multi-cultural, multi-faith place that it is today. There were no mosques and temples on the sky line. There were no great concentrations of people of different faiths who have arrived from other countries. You might have seen the occasional man with a turban in the street, or more probably cleaning on the London Underground, but that did not seem to challenge the latent Christian culture of these islands.

It is a very different matter now. There are far more Muslims than Methodists in Britain, and within a few years it looks as if they will outnumber the Anglicans, too. Muslims, Hindus, Buddhists all have their own holy books, which the adherents treat with far greater reverence, understanding and obedience than the average churchman treats the Bible. It is deemed OK for playwrights and film-makers to make Jesus out to be a homosexual, a revolutionary, or an adulterous lover of Mary Magdalene: there is little complaint. But try that with the prophet Muhammad and see the reaction! Try treating Muslims and Hindus in the same way that they treat Christians in countries where they are in charge, and it becomes very clear that the climate has changed enormously. No privileged position of any sort is given to the Christian church. Any Brownie points it gets are hard-earned.

How, then, can one lead a 'mission' in such a climate? People are unwilling to take anything on authority. They may well be suspicious of any truth claims. They are sure to ask, 'What about other religions and holy books?' They want to discover things for themselves, not to be preached at. They have largely dismissed all thoughts of death and the sequel, setting their minds, instead, on this life and happiness. They are shy of joining any institution or political party – why then should they join that most old-fashioned of institutions, the church? They are used to dismissing advertisers, political promises and other propagandists: why should they listen to a spokesperson from the church? And how are they to regard the central claims of Christianity? A God that seems improbable. A

Jesus comparable to other great teachers. A challenge to repentance and faith which is most unacceptable. Who is telling me to repent and change my lifestyle? And who is telling me what to believe? I will find my own way, thanks very much.

And anyhow, how uninteresting these church people are. Mostly old. Hardly any families or young adults. Services that are dull and do not connect with Monday to Saturday life. Ancient, chilly buildings. Fifteen-minute monologues when even the newscasters these days would not attempt it. Dreary music. And they don't seem to *do* anything. They just go into this building for an hour or so a week and that seems to be it. The majority of the population quite understandably decide to give it a body swerve!

But despite these difficulties there are two things in particular that work in favour of the church, if only we can grasp them. The first is practical. If people can see that the church is *doing* something for the community, their reaction might be quite different. Perhaps it runs a feeding programme for the hungry, or seeks to provide homes for refugees. Perhaps it offers free legal help for the maginalised, or campaigns for playing fields for the teenagers. People are fed up with talk. They want action. After all, deeds speak louder than words. They want to see if Christianity makes any difference. And once they do, they may sit up and take notice. They certainly will not do so if this practical goodness is missing. Our Christianity has for far too long been cerebral (like its Enlightenment background) and not nearly sufficiently earthed or incarnational (like Jesus).

There is a second thing, a very remarkable development in our culture, that can work for the church if only we learn how to run with it. It is this. There is nowadays

a widespread rejection of religion, but an almost universal search for spirituality. 'Your religions teach religion,'
said Shirley Maclaine, 'not spirituality.' There is an enormous interest in spiritual matters of all kinds. I remember
dining with Sir Alister Hardy back in the 1980s and
being fascinated by his discoveries in this area. Leaving
the Chair of Biology at Oxford he set up a centre for
research into the spiritual quest of people in the country.
He was inundated by claims from all over the land from
people who had had some significant sort of 'spiritual
experience'. His work has been developed by others, and
it appears that whereas, as we have seen, church attendance has dropped by some 20 per cent in the last 20
years, reports of spiritual experiences increased by some
60 per cent during the same period. Professor Hay, who
has been researching this at Nottingham University,
claims that his research shows that on a conservative estimate, 76 per cent of the population now say they have
had a clear spiritual experience – such as awareness of
God's presence, the palpable presence of some evil force,
answered prayer, or supposed communication with the
dead.

I was fascinated recently when speaking at a meeting
organised by one of the prime companies in British industry, to find a galaxy of terms being used about the
mission, the vision, the transformation and so forth of
the company – words of course borrowed from the Christian tradition. There are constant advertisements pointing
to the 'new you' and the way in which such and such a
product will give 'enriched life' and 'spiritual growth'.
And of course the masses that are turning to strange cults
and to the practices of the New Age make the same point.
Ours is a culture in search of spiritual fulfilment. God is
out of fashion, morality is questionable, materialism is

desirable but it does not satisfy – so go on the spiritual search! Find what is right for you!

Sadly, most people will not look to the church in order to fulfil this search. It is probably the last place they will look. But what an opportunity it offers us! Many of the objects to which they look for spiritual satisfaction will provide nothing of the sort. If only we could touch that hunger in the human heart we could be in business. And unless we do, no church, no 'mission', is going to make any impact.

Of course, in a society as varied as our own, there is no one worldview we shall meet, no single approach that will suffice. But unless it is manifest that the Christianity we profess makes a real difference to ordinary people, and expresses something of the love and generosity of Jesus Christ, we will get nowhere. Equally, unless we find some way of speaking into the contemporary quest for something that makes life really worth living, we shall fail comprehensively. Jesus came saying, 'I have come that you may have life, life in all its fulness' (John 10:10). That note must be struck by his followers. We will consider some of the helpful approaches for the speaker or preacher in a later chapter. But first we must say something about the church that is asking for a mission.

3

The Honey Pot and the Rose – Where can we find them?

You only have to go out into the garden for a picnic, and open a honey pot, and you get inundated with wasps. They do not have to be invited, let alone drummed up. They simply come, drawn by the attractiveness of the honey. You only have to have a fragrant rose in bloom in your garden for people to stop and smell it. You don't have to ask them, bribe them or cajole them. Something arresting and attractive is before them. They respond. Surely that is the message *par excellence* for the Christian church. If it is to grow, it must prove attractive to non-members.

But alas that is often not the case. As I write the Roman Catholic Church throughout much of North America (and a little earlier in Canada) is being revealed as a haven for priests who sexually abuse young boys. In Canada the Anglican Church is, along with the Federal Government, being brought to book for the ill-fated attempts to turn Indians into 'real' Canadians by wresting them from their homes at an early age, forcing them into boarding schools, forbidding them to speak their own language and inflicting all manner of abuse, verbal, physical and sexual, on them. Is it any wonder that they are turned off the church?

Most people have horror stories about the church, and we Christians try to distance ourselves from them. But we know in our hearts that even our own local church is not a honey pot or a rose. It does not intrigue and attract. Perhaps we would be wise to go back to square one and see how the earliest Christians made such a hit that we read 'the common people heard them gladly' and were 'daily added to their number'. What made them a honey pot?

Basically, of course, we must go back to Jesus. What made him so attractive? He was not a professional religious man, not an authorised rabbinic teacher. He was an ordinary working man. But there was something utterly unique about him: his behaviour completely matched his words. There is a marvellous strand in the Fourth Gospel which tells us that God pursued his mission to the world by sending Jesus: and Jesus made God known by his words and deeds – his teaching and his works of love went hand in hand. All of this shows the glory of God. It reveals in brilliant, attractive light what Ultimate Reality is like. All kinds of people are drawn to it, unless they are determined to stay in the dark. We could point to his utter unselfishness: living in poverty, giving his all, loving all and sundry, healing and meeting need even when exhausted, and eventually pouring out his lifeblood in death after being falsely accused. Such undeserved love, love without strings, is immensely appealing. Or we could look at his sheer vitality – combining youth, activity, wisdom, with wonderful promises of what he could do in the lives of men and women who entrusted themselves to him. We could go on endlessly drawing out the characteristics of Jesus, because he is the most winsome person who has ever lived.

But let us instead turn to those we feel are more on our own level, the first Christians. What did they have that made them so attractive? How come they 'turned the world upside down' (Acts 17:6)? They had no church buildings, to be sure. No money behind them. No training apart from three years following the Master. They had no rabbinic education, and were not part of the religious establishment. The ancient world was full of philosophies, and gripped by even more variant lifestyles than we have in our own day. What made the Christians stand out? If we can discover that, and transpose it into our own situation, we may begin to see some of the qualities that give fragrance to the rose!

First, it was a community thing. The sheer quality of Christian community was immensely attractive. It embraced rich and poor, slaves and free, old and young, Jew and Greek. It all began with Jesus, of course. His coming to preach the kingdom of God began with calling a very mixed bunch of fishermen, freedom fighters, mystics, and ordinary men and women to follow him in close companionship. They found him irresistible. They had found treasure, and it showed. So we do not need to rely only on the passages at the end of Acts 2 and Acts 4 where we read of the fellowship, the joy, the prayer and the mutual generosity of the first disciples. It is evident in the very words they used to describe their movement. It was an army in which all were soldiers. It was a family in which all were children. It was a body in which all were limbs. It was a building in which all were stones. It was a loaf in which all were ingredients. There is no sniff of the 'lone ranger' idea of an evangelist in the New Testament. Evangelism – that is to say being the honey pot, embodying the fragrance of the rose – is the task of the whole church. So you don't have to try too hard, and put on endless programmes. You have to live a life of loving commitment to one another, a partnership which eclipses the fellowship of the pub down the road. Usually, alas, the pub has a lot more of that committed, enjoyable partnership than the church. But many people find ours is a lonely world. And a church which really does embody that love, that mutual support, is immensely attractive.

Second, it was a generosity thing. The God they had come to know through Jesus is sheer generosity, and they mirrored it in countless ways. In the way they shared their possessions. In their care for the hungry. In their welcome of strangers, Gentiles, centurions and slaves. In their concern for the welfare of shipwrecked soldiers. In their determination to help a jailor, rather than escape, when his prison had been split open by an earthquake. In their prayer for those in prison. In their offer of eternal life to their judges and persecutors. These people were full of amazing generosity. It is a highly attractive quality. When people feel themselves to be on the receiving end of a generosity they have done nothing to deserve, that tends to wake them up, not least in a rather selfish age such as our own. Does your church glow with generosity to all and sundry? Does it embody the uncalculating generosity of God, whether people respond or whether they do not? If so, it is sure to prove a honey pot, because behaviour like that is rare.

I think of a girl who came up to Oxford, where I was working as a clergyman. She developed anorexia nervosa, and, despite the best medical attention, seemed likely to die. The Christian fellowship in her College determined to stay with her day and night, encouraging her, cheering her up, making her laugh, and feeding her when she could bear it. They took it in turns to sleep on her floor.

The result? Before long she came back to full life and health. And it was no surprise that she became a follower of the Jesus who had inspired in these fellow students such love and generosity of spirit.

Third, it was a worship thing. Another quality that emerges from the pages of the New Testament about these Christians was their dynamic worship. Worship in the ancient world was pretty dull, rather like many a church today. It was predictable. It was done by the professionals. Most of the worshippers did not believe in the ancient gods to whom the offerings were made. Not so very different from some situations today. But here were these people using psalms and hymns and spiritual songs, making melody in their hearts to the Lord. They feasted on the ancient scriptures and showed their relevance to contemporary life. They gave themselves to heartfelt prayer, and experienced many answers to those prayers. Worship did not rest in the hands of the professionals (not that they had any!). 'When you come together, each one has a hymn, a lesson, a revelation, a tongue or an interpretation' (1 Corinthians 14:26). I know of churches like that – not enough of them, but some. And they draw people. They become a focus for the spiritual hunger that is part of today's world. Praise, joy, teaching, love, prayer and gratitude to the living God – it is a heady mixture. It is magnetic.

Fourth, it was a conviction thing. These first Christians were passionate in their conviction, and not afraid to show it. They were utterly persuaded that Jesus was the Saviour of the world, and they were not embarrassed at all to speak of him and if necessary suffer and die for him. You could reject them, but they bounced back. You could scorn them, but they kept on praising that crucified carpenter of theirs. You could imprison them, but they converted their captors. You could kill them, but they died with praises on their lips. They were utterly persuaded that in Jesus they had found treasure and they were keen for others to share it. Very hard to contend with, then or now!

Fifth, it was a missionary thing. And by 'missionary' I do not just mean those courageous men and women who go to other lands with the gospel – people from whom the ordinary run of Christians tend to distance themselves. No, in those days the temperature at the heart of the church seems to have been so warm that normal, regular members could not help being missionaries by telling others of the Saviour who had transformed their own lives. We see from the New Testament that many of these people were fishermen, ex-prostitutes, business people, tamed men of violence, erstwhile drunkards, reformed sexual perverts, soldiers – in fact ordinary people of every kind. And they proved so passionate to chat to others about Jesus that the first church historian, Eusebius, tells us that they journeyed to nearby towns and villages to pass on the good news of the One who had made new people of them.

Evangelism was not a thing that some specialists did to people. It was not something beyond the sea, though it included that. No, it was the supreme passion of the average church member. A glance through the Acts of the Apostles will show that the twelve apostles were less prominently involved than little mission teams, leading open air witness by a river, working in prisons, teaching in synagogues, at the street corners, or even in the desert. These people were like a Kansas dust storm. You simply cannot keep it out. And it was this passion to make Jesus known that proved so arresting, and so attractive. These days this is, sadly, very unusual in the West. But in the developing world where the faith is growing so fast, it is commonplace. Freely they have received the good news of a Saviour. Freely they give him away.

There were undoubtedly other factors that made these first Christians stand out. But these five were central, and they are all immensely attractive. If you have churches today where the membership as a whole is convinced about Jesus and excited with him; if you have a unity and love which it is hard to find anywhere else; if you find a caring for non-members which is extraordinary in its generosity; if you find worship that takes you out of yourself and challenges you to find a convincing explanation; and if you have ordinary Christians who cannot keep quiet about Jesus; then you have the sort of church where mission is a way of life and 'an evangelistic mission' is likely to prove fruitful!

The Practicalities

4

The Message –
What is good news for today?

There is a very curious thing about Christianity compared with most other religions: it is inescapably a missionary faith. Though it has a few Trappist monks among its members, it is essentially a community with a message to proclaim. That is not because we belong, as E. M. Forster once put it, to 'poor little talkative Christianity', though that rebuke is sometimes just, but because every Christian is called, in virtue of conversion, to a missionary God, to share in God's loving action for the world in some way or other. This does not mean that all should become preachers. What a disaster that would be! But it does mean that there are meant to be no drones in the Christian hive. All are called to work in some way or other, and according to their gifting, within the *missio Dei* that we thought about at the start of this book.

After all, if you have found good news, you are duty-bound to pass it on. What would we think of someone who developed the vaccine against AIDS and enjoyed its immunity without ever sharing it with others? To be a Christian is necessarily to be involved in God's mission. And that includes *verbal* involvement. Many people tell

43

me that theirs is a silent witness dependent on the way they live their lives. That is great from one point of view. Without a godly life our beliefs mean nothing to outsiders. But it is totally inadequate. Just think what it would have been like had Jesus just lived his matchless life, but said nothing! The early church would never have got off the ground if Peter had stood up on the Day of Pentecost and said, 'We have nothing to proclaim: but take a look at our lifestyle.' In any case, who among us is going to put their lives up as the model of what Christians should be? And even if we did, people might just get the impression that we were quite nice people, rather than those in the process of being transformed by a divine power. We have something crucial to declare, and must find the best way to do it in an age that is sceptical about God, cynical about truth and unimpressed by ethical demands.

It is the responsibility of all Christians to be able to say something about Jesus Christ and the difference he makes in their lives. The New Testament calls this 'witness', and it is the job of us all. But what about those who have the gift of the 'evangelist', 'the good news person'? We will leave the preparation of evangelistic talks and sermons until the next chapter. Here I will focus on the message itself. What do we have to proclaim, and how can we do it in such a way as to pierce the contemporary armour of apathy and unbelief? What follows is no complete answer, but some suggestions I have found helpful.

The element of surprise

People think they know what Christianity is, and they have dismissed it as puerile, irrelevant, antiquated or just one of the many religious myths. They have no idea of its radical nature. It was rather like that in the time of Jesus. People knew what both Jewish and Roman religion was about, and they were either bored, or nominal, or passionate about it. The outstanding thing that comes to me through the Gospels is that the good news brought by Jesus was entirely unexpected. It revolutionised people's understanding. Vast crowds dropped tools and took days off to go and listen to this carpenter. The Jews had been discussing the kingdom of God for decades, with many different views of what it would entail, generally involving kicking out the Romans from the Holy Land and restoring Israel's glory. The truly amazing thing about Jesus' initial words, as we find them in Mark 1:15, is the confident note of fulfilment: 'the time is fulfilled and the kingdom of God is at hand'. Not future bliss but here-and-now reality. It was present, because Jesus brought it in. Truly staggering news, and almost incredible, coming as it did from this Galilean peasant.

The 'kingdom of God' has various meanings: it draws attention to God's rightful claims on his world as our King; it comes to mean those who acknowledge his kingly rule in their lives. And so 'entering the kingdom' or 'receiving the kingdom', words that were so often on Jesus' lips, essentially means making God King, putting him in the number one slot in life. It was a radical challenge to the nation and to individuals alike.

Of course, not everyone believed him. There was plenty of scepticism and opposition, culminating in the crucifixion. But his message of the kingdom did not change. It was central. And he backed his claims to usher in the kingdom by kingdom works (healings, miracles, acts of love) and kingdom people (the twelve apostles representing the twelve tribes of the original Israel, and demonstrating that close community which comes about when people make God their King). Kingdom works and kingdom people remain major factors validating his claims on human allegiance.

The kingly claims of the living God are certainly no more acceptable now than they were then. Particularly in a postmodern world, kingship and all authority structures smack of ruthless power, determined to achieve its will, imposing it on others. We cannot change the message, though we must interpret it. The God whom we present is not the God whom Feuerbach and Nietzsche reacted so strongly against. He is no ruthless despot who demands obedience to his will. He is the supreme Lover, the one who sacrifices himself for those he calls to acknowledge his rightful place. He is the generous King who invites all and sundry into his party, and even offers them the clothes to cover their inadequacies and enable them to enjoy it. In an age when 'god' can mean anything from the natural world to Shirley Maclaine, we Christians are called to present the claims of a transcendent, living God, the author of all there is, and declare that so far from wanting to dominate and regiment us he offers joy and fulfilment when we entrust our lives to him. That is a big surprise, and I find that when people discover that Christianity is not what they thought it was, they often sit up and take notice.

The source of our frustrations

In days gone by it was normal to conceive of God as the moral ruler of the universe. It followed that every one of us was in deep trouble with him. We had failed to do many good things. We had done many bad things. Ours was an attitude of rebellion. We were guilty and in desperate need of rescue. The situation has not changed, but our presentation of it must, if we are to win a hearing. For many people are utterly unaware of 'sin'. It involves the concept of a holy God which they may never even have considered, let alone credited. It means that there is some ultimate standard by which we are judged – and both ideas are repugnant. We do not see ourselves as guilty, but merely as frustrated, overwhelmed by circumstances, the victims of society and so forth.

The task of the evangelist is gently and with many contemporary illustrations to bring home to people that their frustrations are the fruit of what Kierkegaard called 'being in the wrong with God'. If the building site of our world and our lives is a mess, this is because we have rejected the architect's instructions. People will understand that: it makes sense. It covers the things that people know are wrong, like rape of the environment, paedophilia, racism and so on. And it points to the cause of more personal areas of frustration and disenchantment in individual lives. One could go further. Most people these days feel not guilt (because that implies a holy personal God whom we have offended, and they are not sure about that) but alienation. The evangelist can point out that we do not only *feel* alienation: we *are* alienated, by the way we have gone our own way and left God out of our lives. It is not difficult for the speaker to show how culpable this attitude of rebellion is against the God who gave us life and lavished his love upon us in the coming and dying and rising of Jesus. We are to blame. We are indeed guilty, not so much for the smaller peccadilloes of our lives but for the great central theme of declaring independence against the God who gave us everything. It is monstrous ingratitude, and God cannot pretend all is well.

It does not matter overmuch if they say that they do not believe in God. Tell them that you are not yet asking them to believe in God, only to listen attentively to what the good news of the gospel is saying, and try it for size. We cannot prove it: our job is to make it plain. But it has its own marvellous power of persuasion!

Getting it together

It is plain that the major problem for humanity is dislocation from God, which has its effect in dislocations of all sorts between human beings. Something radical is needed that will get to the root of our condition. And the marvellous good news is that God does not patronise us, pretending that we are great folk: he does not stand over us telling us to keep this, that and the other command. He wants us to see that his attitude towards us is holy love. Holy, because he cannot bear for us to stay in the alienation we have chosen. Love, because he is prepared himself to bear its awesome consequences.

This leads you directly to speak of Jesus who is, as Irenaeus put it long ago, 'the kingdom in person'. He is the one who brings to us God's challenge and God's succour. His name is Jesus – 'God to the rescue'. That rescue began when he became one of us at Bethlehem. It continued as he demonstrated in his life and ministry what it could mean to live under God's kingly rule. And it came to its climax when he gave himself on the cross to erase the results of our alienation by his self-giving, and to bring us back, forgiven and able to stand tall before the God we had so hurt and insulted. Nor was Calvary the end of it. He rose triumphant from the grip of death, alive for evermore. He is the risen one. And he meets us, as he met many at the conclusion of the gospel story, inviting them to surrender their lives to him. Thomas the doubter then fell at his feet and led the way by calling Jesus 'My Lord and my God'.

That and nothing less is the journey we are all called to take. Jesus is the one who reconciles us with the heavenly Father. We only come to the Father through him, for he alone has embodied the Father's love, self-sacrifice and welcome. Our task is to show people that God himself has done everything necessary to put us right with him, and that we can, from the very moment we close with his offer, begin to live life as it was intended. And that means life in touch with God, pleasing him and enjoying his company. If we can present this to people we shall have done well!

Flexibility

There are many ways of presenting this undreamed-of good news that God is not against us but for us and has done everything to put us in the right with him. As John Bowen points out in his superb new book *Evangelism for 'Normal' People*, St Paul uses a variety of images in a single context to bring home what God has done. In 2 Corinthians 5:15 it is the picture of a brand new life which God offers to the spiritually dead; in verse 19 it is 'reconciliation' or the breaking down of barriers to fellowship, and in verse 21 it is substitution: 'For our sake God made Christ to be sin, who knew no sin, so that in him we might be made the righteousness of God.' Wonderful flexibility! Resurrection language in the first instance, relationship language in the second, and religious language (sin and atonement) in the third. But a pattern runs through these three very different images. The picture may be different but the message is the same. In each case we find Paul maintaining that humankind is in the wrong.

- We experience a kind of death.
- We are alienated and need reconciliation.
- We need forgiveness.

Furthermore, each of the three, as Bowen observes, speaks of Jesus as the solution to the problem.

- Jesus was resurrected and offers the new life.
- Jesus is the means of our reconciliation.
- Christ the sinless one became sin for us.

One could go further. Each one talks of an exchange: Christ gives us something and we give him something.

- We give Christ our death and he gives his resurrection life.
- We give him our alienation from God and he gives us his relationship with God.
- We give him our sin and he gives us his righteousness.

Here we see Paul, the master evangelist, sensitively and flexibly varying his imagery so that it speaks to as wide a circle as possible, while remaining consistent on the core of his message: human failure, divine restoration, and the need for a step. It is a great lesson for the preacher!

Invitation

Many preachers are shy about mentioning the need for a step of commitment. It seems too embarrassing, too intrusive. But it is part of our commission. Jesus did it. The apostles did it. The preachers down the ages did it. So must we. We must insist on the need for a step of encounter with God, of reaching out to the one who

reaches out to us. Of course, there are those so-called
evangelists who are always frothing at the mouth and
crying out for decision, often at inappropriate times. But
abuse does not take away proper use. And it is obvious
that if God offers us life, we must choose it. If he calls us
to be reconciled, we must decide whether to respond or
not. If he offers us Christ's sinless status since Christ has
taken ours, we must decide whether or not to say an
adoring 'Yes, please'.

What evangelists are not entitled to do is to insist that
it must be 'now, now'. We may invite them, challenge
them, but it is the work of the Holy Spirit to bring people
to that response in his own time. But we must make it
very plain that everyone is called to respond to God's
loving generosity. There is great emphasis in today's evangelism on process rather than crisis. Of course there is a
process: many people know so little about the gospel that
it would be impossible for them to respond the first time
they heard it. But at some time in the process there needs
to be a crisis: the crisis of falling into the arms of the
great Lover. We may not even be aware of quite when it
has happened. All we know is that, like the Prodigal Son,
we have come home.

Suddenness is no necessary part of the gospel, but
commitment is. We are all on a journey. The task of the
evangelist is to turn those who are moving away from
Christ to start moving towards him. Somewhere along
the journey, there will be a crisis.

It is just the same in human relationships. Very few
people propose the first time they go out with someone!
It takes time, reflection and growing acquaintance before
the man and the woman are ready to plunge into a lifelong commitment.

That is not my daring metaphor: the image of the bride

of Christ is one the New Testament loves. He is the Bride-groom, we are the bride. It is as if the Father looks at the Saviour and asks, 'Will you have this sinner to be yours for ever, to have and to hold until not even death can part you?' And Jesus stretches out his arms, as they were stretched upon the cross, and says, 'I will.' But that does not make us married! Not until we respond to God's gentle question, 'Sinner, will you have this Saviour to be yours for ever, to have and to hold until not even death can part you?' and joyfully whisper 'I will.'

There is the repentance, the turning from the old way of life, which Christ requires of us. There is the faith, the adoring trust in the one who welcomes us. And, as in marriage, the two parties are made one. That act of surrender is the beginning of the new life together. Baptism is the wedding ring, the physical mark of belonging to that new relationship. There is a whole lifetime together stretching ahead. Now they are no longer sep-arated but united; no longer alienated but reconciled. The old has gone. The new life has begun.

It is the task of the preacher, not least in a mission situation, to stress the importance of that step, whether the response comes then or later. It is also the preacher's responsibility to make clear the costly, lifelong nature of this union, and the means for developing it in appropriate nurture and discipleship. But more of that in a later chapter. The evangelist needs not only to surprise and excite his hearers, not only to translate biblical concepts into contemporary ones without distortion, not only to point to the source of our frustrations and what God has done about it, but also gently yet firmly to remind his hearers that they must choose.

5

The Good News –
How shall we tell it?

It was Phillips Brooks who declared that preaching was truth through personality. So it is. And every preacher should make use of the God-given personality he or she has, so it is not possible to lay down in detail how preachers of the good news should operate. But certain principles apply to all good evangelistic preaching. Perhaps we can approach them through a series of questions.

Why bother?

Why indeed? Many preachers do not bother to evangelise. There is a dearth of good relevant evangelism in our churches today. But surely the love of God, who so loved the world that he gave his only Son, must drive us into mission. If we are Christians at all, we must take seriously both the great commandment of Jesus, to love the Lord and our neighbour with everything we have got, and also the Great Commission of Jesus, to go and make disciples worldwide. Moreover, it is very apparent that there is a profound need for the gospel all over the world, not least in our own country. It is also an enormous privilege: God seems not to have entrusted the preaching of the gospel to angels or even to highly gifted human beings unless they have been to the cross for forgiveness. Then it is their responsibility to pass on what they have received. What is more, it is a tremendous joy. To stand there holding out the promise of life at its best to people, and seeing faces attentive to the good news – why, there is nothing on earth to beat it!

What are the pathways to effective gospel proclamation?

First, I must believe in preaching. I must see it as a God-given way of bringing people to know him. I must believe in the power of this strange activity, and expect God to act through it.

Second, I must trust the Scriptures. All great preaching down the ages has been biblical preaching. We are not at liberty to alter the terms of our commissions. As we open up the meaning of the Bible passage we can expect the Holy Spirit to use it to convict and convert, to nourish and to teach in a way our words simply cannot. Whole denominations have moved away from biblical preaching, and consistently these are the ones losing most members. All over the world, the churches that proclaim the message of the Bible, and believe it, are growing. Certainly the power of the biblical message to transform lives is undeniable. This does not mean we must shout at people in the King James version, or always begin the preaching by announcing a text. But it does mean that the content of our proclamation will make use of and be in line with the thrust of Holy Scripture.

Third, I must make Jesus central to all I have to say. He is the Bread of Life. He is the Way, the Truth and the Life. Most of all, people need to hear him, see him, feed on him and receive him. It is not surprising, therefore, that addresses which major on Jesus are usually the most effective in drawing people to him. It is vital to show people what he is really like, and what he has done for us. I need to make plain the cost of following him and the way to find him.

Fourth, I must build bridges. Bridges between what is so clear to me and so obscure to my hearers. Bridges between the New Testament and the contemporary situation. Bridges between God's agenda and ours. We are called, if we are preachers, to be bridge-builders, with one end of the bridge firmly anchored to the New Testament and the other planted equally firmly into the culture and the concerns of our hearers.

Fifth, I must be definite, bold, and yet vulnerable in my preaching. Definite in content, aim, thought, language and expectancy. I must be bold, unafraid of the vested interests which my hearers may cherish, bold in preaching for a verdict. But I must be vulnerable, too, and show that I am a poor weak sinner grasped by a mighty God and struggling to make him known. And I must expect the sermon to achieve something.

What attracts people to Jesus?

If Jesus is the human face of God, we should not be surprised that people are drawn to him for all manner of reasons. This is particularly the case in the multi-cultural postmodern age in which we live. But I believe St John gives us some broad categories for understanding what attracts many to Jesus – this was indeed the aim of his Gospel (20:31).

For some it is the sense of *discovery*. You see it in Andrew (John 1:40–42). He was so thrilled with what he had discovered about Jesus that he dragged Simon Peter his brother to meet him. When people have made a life-changing discovery in this rather jaded world, it attracts attention, and others want to know. That is why so often new believers are the best evangelists. They have so many friends who are not Christians, and the difference Jesus is beginning to make in their lives invites curiosity.

For some it is the sense of *wonder*. That is what struck the disciples when Jesus turned water into wine (John 2:11). When people are caught up in wonder, love and praise as they worship God, it shows in their body language and their faces, and has an enormous power to attract. When the water of a very ordinary life is transformed by the Spirit this also often elicits in others a sense of wonder and hunger to know more.

For some it is the sense of *being loved*. That attracts to Jesus like nothing on earth. John 3:16 is archetypal. If people see themselves as the recipients of a love that sought them and sacrificed for them when they were in total rebellion, that has its own marvellous way of melting hearts.

Sometimes it is the sense of *power* that draws people. It often did in response to the miracles of Jesus (e.g. John 5:1–18). Today, particularly in the Two Thirds World, many are drawn to Jesus from other faiths by this means. Perhaps through a vision of Jesus, perhaps through a dream, perhaps through a healing. The sheer power of the Lord draws them.

Sometimes it is a sense of *gratitude*. It was so with the man blind from birth whom Jesus healed in John chapter 9. The overwhelming sense of what God in Christ has done for us, at such tremendous cost, draws many to respond in gratitude. I guess the worst moment for an atheist is when he is full of gratitude and has nobody to thank!

Sometimes people are won because of a sense of *need*. That comes through strongly in the contrasting stories of Nicodemus (John 3) and the woman at the well (John 4). Both were in need, and came to see it. That sense of need is a powerful factor in many people today. It may be for forgiveness, as it was with the woman taken in adultery (John 8:1–11). But it may be the need for significance, for power over destructive habits, for companionship, for meaning in a world that seems devoid of it. There are many shapes of human need, and some people are drawn through seeing that Jesus can meet that crying need of theirs.

How can we prepare the address?

A good evangelistic address is crisp: it wastes no words. It is interesting: it grabs attention from the opening sentence and maintains it throughout. It is biblical: Scripture has a power our words do not. It is relevant to the needs of the hearers, and is immediately perceived to be so. And it challenges people to decision.

Here are seven of the things I try to bear in mind as I prepare. It often helps to think of one individual who is not yet a Christian and has promised me he will be there.

Start where they are

It is important that the content of our preaching is biblical, but it is usually a mistake to start with a text of Scripture. You need to get the taste buds working first! Start where they are. That is good educational method. I wrote a book some time ago called *You Must Be Joking*, and the chapter headings were all things I had heard people say; things which lent themselves to an evangelistic talk, like 'You can't believe in God these days', 'All religions lead to God', 'When you're dead, you're dead' and so forth. Those titles and that book have had a continuing interest and appeal because they are addressed to questions real people are asking.

There are many ways you can capture interest with your title. You can take an assumption and destroy it: 'It doesn't matter what you believe so long as you are sincere'. You can take a theme and develop it: I remember speaking evangelistically at a Valentine's party, on 'Love: our Number One interest'. You can take a modern concern: 'How to be married and stay that way', or, more boldly, 'How to sleep with the same partner for 50 years'! You can take a perennial fascination and give it a new twist: 'Is there life before death?' You can intrigue by humour: I remember preaching an evangelistic sermon to Oxford students on 'Marx is dead, God is dead, and I'm not feeling too good myself'!

It is often wise to key in to a contemporary feeling. I shall never forget the power I unwittingly discovered and released when I stumbled upon the subject of 'Choose freedom' in Africa, as it was beginning to become the subject of the continent. In the days of student attraction to Marxism I found subjects like 'The revolutionary Jesus' drew large numbers in the universities. Of course, if you are going to tackle subjects like that you really have to do them full justice or people will rightly feel cheated. On that occasion I recall contrasting the thoughts of Chairman Mao with the words of Jesus in the Sermon on the Mount.

One further word about maintaining interest. I find it very helpful to use testimony and drama in the course of a talk. They are both capable of standing on their own, of course, but make a strong impact when introduced into the heart of a talk. The change of voice, of pace, of impact is usually very effective.

Attend to translation

As we saw, the 'kingdom of God' was a major theme in the Synoptic Gospels, but in the Fourth Gospel, designed for use primarily in Greek culture, we find 'eternal life' largely replacing kingdom language. The content is very much the same, but the form of expression is entirely different, because it was designed to connect with a very different community. We find the apostle Paul doing much the same thing in his letter to the Colossians. Christian evangelism always involves translation, not only of language but of thought forms. After all, if God translated himself into a human being, and a Jewish carpenter at that, we should not be afraid of translation. But it is difficult. Stick too woodenly to the original concept and you will fail to communicate with the new situation. Move too far away from it and you will no longer be true to its message.

One of the most illuminating books on this topic I have ever read, and one which has enormously influenced me in my own attempts to translate the concepts of the good news without evacuating their meaning and challenge, is *Peace Child* by Don and Carol Richardson. These Canadian missionaries set out to evangelise the Sawi tribespeople in an unreached part of Borneo. They discovered to their horror that every known virtue was despised as a vice in Sawi culture. When the tribesmen heard the story of the passion, and how Judas betrayed Jesus with a kiss, he immediately became the supreme hero in their eyes, because treachery under the guise of friendship was seen as the highest of virtues! How do you preach the gospel in an upside-down culture like that?

The missionaries were very perplexed, until they came across a strange custom: the Peace Child. When the Sawi wanted to restore trust with other tribes after a war, the heads of each tribe would exchange their precious babies, as the guarantee of peace between them. The most heinous of all crimes was to kill the Peace Child, for then another bloody war would ensue. The Richardsons saw that this was the way in. They told how God had given his Peace Child because he wanted to make peace with us, and how human beings had actually killed the Peace Child. But instead of wiping us out in vengeance, God had raised him from the dead: he is alive and able to guarantee peace between God and those who trust him. Gradually the message sank in, and Judas was no longer the hero, evil was no longer the goal, and the spread of the gospel among the Sawi was remarkable. The Richardsons had learnt a crucial lesson in translation. They had clothed the good news in the language and culture of those to whom they were speaking.

That is the preacher's task. It is demanding work, but immensely satisfying when we find that our message deeply resonates with our audience. I find that in today's postmodern society the language of relationship, of meaning and purpose in life, of personal identity (who am I?), of value (what am I worth?) and of destiny (where am I headed?) are particularly relevant, and I am increasingly seeing the gospel in terms of what it means to be a human being in the light of all the dehumanising influences around us. I often find that the language of the more thoughtful and successful pop songs poses the questions that come straight from the heart: the gospel speaks direct to them. Naturally, the songs you choose to quote will be determined to a large extent by the expected age range of your audience.

Shape your material

This is not a book about preaching, but there are a number of things to keep in mind for an evangelistic address.

First, your aim. You should have a crystal clear, single aim which governs all you have to say. If not, you will be surprised how good people are at missing the point altogether.

Second, your plan. Break the material up so that your hearers can easily latch on to what you are saying. Make it palatable. Have clear headings. And make sure that every point subserves and reinforces the aim of the whole address.

Third, your illustrations. These are crucially important. They act as windows and let the light in. They make the obscure clear, the abstract concrete. The TV, films, the local paper, songs and your own observations of life all furnish good material for illustrations.

Fourth, your start and conclusion are critical. If you lose people in the first minute you will never get them back. And if, like an aeroplane circling Heathrow, you cannot land, you will fail comprehensively in your evangelism. The ending should be the final hammer blow to drive home the theme of the whole sermon.

Be Christ-centred

Speak much of him. He is the supremely attractive one. He promised that if he were lifted up from the earth he would draw all kinds of people to him. And he does. So we need to major on who he is, what he has done, and particularly the point people find hard to take in, that this Jesus is alive and willing to share our very lives if we will let him. The early Christians had an outline in those

Acts sermons which they used a good deal. It was a wise one. They spoke to a need, once they discerned it. They told of a person, Jesus the Saviour. They proffered the twin gifts of forgiveness and the Holy Spirit. And they looked for a response, a tangible response of repentance, faith and baptism into the Christian community. We could profitably follow their example.

Watch the balance

The gospel of Christ is large and broad. It is easy to miss great areas of it because we have tunnel vision on other aspects. John Stott, himself a brilliant evangelistic preacher, has drawn attention to seven New Testament explanations of the gospel, which fit different audiences.

- *Sacrificial* – the shedding and sprinkling of Christ's blood.
- *Messianic* – the breaking in of the age of God's promised rule.
- *Mystic* – the receiving of eternal life and being in Christ.
- *Legal* – the righteous judge pronouncing the unrighteous forgiven.
- *Personal* – the Father reconciling his wayward children.
- *Salvific* – divine liberation for his oppressed people: the new exodus.
- *Cosmic* – the Lord claiming universal dominion over the powers.

It is easy to shrink the gospel. Balance is needed. That is where discerning friends can be a help to us. Evangelism without much doctrine, with no mention of the cost of discipleship, with no depth, no warmth, no social content and no sensitivity, is a travesty of the real thing. Critique from wise friends and a wide understanding of Scripture provide the remedy.

Bathe it in prayer

This is the most important part of preparation for an evangelistic event. Pray for it yourself. Get your fellow leaders to pray for you. Make it a topic of prayer at the prayer meeting. Prayer burns the message into you. Prayer will burn it into the souls of some who hear you. Prayer facilitates the work of the Spirit, taking home the Scripture he inspired that you are speaking about. Prayer shows God we depend utterly on him, not on our own efforts. I love the words of an old Cornish Methodist local preacher on the subject of preparing a sermon: 'First, I reads myself full; then, I thinks myself clear; then I prays myself hot; then I lets go!'

Plan the conclusion

This is by far the hardest part, and I am rarely satisfied that I have made the most of it. But here are some suggestions from my own experience, which may be of some small help.

Only challenge for response when you have said at least something in the course of your address about the need, the cross and resurrection, the cost, and the availability of the Holy Spirit. Otherwise your challenge is more or less empty.

Give yourself time to handle this part of the talk properly. Do not allow yourself to get squeezed by preaching too long before then. You need time to pause, to let the importance of it all sink in.

Learn to plead with people. This is rare nowadays, but important. We do not merely want to inform the mind or convict the conscience. We want the warmth of Jesus, the seriousness of the issues, and the awesome alternative to coming to Christ to be reflected in what we say at this juncture.

Watch people's faces and try to read their minds. It is not as difficult as it might seem. Learn to respond to questions which may be in their minds: 'Are you wondering what it will cost to follow Christ? Let me try to answer that question.' This divining of what is going on in your audience and speaking directly and succinctly into it is immensely powerful. Ask God for the gift.

Your attitude should be a mixture of being bold and fearless on the one hand, and warm and gentle on the other. Trust the Word of God. It is powerful. Placard the promises of God and the cross of Christ before the eyes of your hearers. They need time, and you need clarity, if they are to take it in.

Use appropriate illustrations at this sensitive time. I find that the best ones are drawn from personal relationships – marriage, coming to a person, throwing oneself into his arms, saying sorry, coming home, opening the door to someone who wants to come in.

Do be clear in what you are asking people to do. People easily get confused at this point. It may be that you are asking them to read a gospel with an open mind to test out its truth for themselves. If so, stay with that goal, and make sure you have a pile of gospels in a modern translation for them to take away. It may be an offer to join an Alpha or similar group: in that case have an invitation to Alpha on every seat. It may be a call to come to Christ then and there. In which case have a response card and pen available for everyone. It may be that you are asking people to go away and think about it and then, if they want to take it further, to come to a talk on Christian assurance in the very near future. In which case make sure the date and place are on the news-sheet that they take away, and that they indicate their intention on the response card.

There are many ways of ending an address, but always seek a response to the challenge of the good news in some way or other. That is what an evangelist is for, after all! Evangelists do not merely teach the faith. They precipitate decision.

But there are many dangers to avoid. Do not press people unduly: that is the Holy Spirit's work, not yours. Do not whip up an emotional atmosphere. You are concerned with their will, not their emotions. Do not manipulate people, but give them ample freedom: after all, God does. Do not suggest that now is the last time they will have the chance to respond. In the mercy of God there may be many more. Be sensitive to the people who have problems and frankly cannot go the whole hog. Sometimes I find it helpful to say, 'You don't understand it all? Neither do I. But how about giving as much of yourself as you are aware of to as much of the Lord as you can believe in? That is quite enough to get started.'

I often end with a full minute of silence while I ask people to think over what their response to the message will be. I sometimes then offer a model prayer of commitment for them to echo, but emphasise that it is only a suggestion to help those who know this is the time to get it sorted out, and don't know how to express it. Then whether or not there is a closing hymn, I invite people who have been helped by the evening to come to a side chapel or somewhere convenient and unobtrusive and pray with members of the team. This is all part of the partnership in the gospel that a team embodies.

I like to offer a little booklet on coming to faith to

people who respond: some find it very helpful to reflect on what they have heard, at their own pace and in cold print. I always want to take their names and addresses or phone numbers and I am quite up-front about this. I point out that it would be quite irresponsible of me to invite people to take such a momentous decision and have no plans to help them on in the faith. So a nurture group needs to be already in place, with the venue and the timing written on the news-sheet or card that I place in their hands.

There is likely to be a good deal of varied and untidy activity at the end of an evangelistic service, with people moving about, writing their names, talking and praying. This is a great advantage. It enables those who have been touched to approach a team member without embarrassment, or stay seated while one of the team comes to join them. An enormous amount of the work of the mission goes on at the end of addresses like these, and this all needs to be meticulously planned and yet handled in a very relaxed way.

I do not want to leave this chapter without emphasising again the importance of prayer. Reconciliation is God's work, and graciously he sometimes allows us to have a share in it. We can by ourselves achieve nothing. So any man-centredness in evangelism is reprehensible. We need to be as hidden as possible, even as speakers. Sometimes we will see little or no response. That is OK. It is God's mission, not ours. But from time to time we shall see God powerfully at work, and marvel. And we shall go to bed profoundly grateful to God, who allows us a small part in his mission to humankind.

6

Personal Evangelism –
How shall we do it?

There is no way that in a single chapter I can do more than give some very simple suggestions on the way one might proceed in talking to an individual after a mission event. The subject of personal evangelism at large is highly sensitive and requires much tact. It involves building bridges of relationship and friendship, seeking opportunities to start a conversation naturally, helping the person to understand the good news, encouraging them to respond to it, and handling attendant difficulties and objections. It also involves aftercare. I have tried to write much more extensively on this subject in *Sharing Your Faith with a Friend* (IVP, 2002). I would also like to recommend James Lawrence, *Lost for Words* (BRF, 1999) and Bill Hybels, *Becoming a Contagious Christian* (Zondervan, 1994). During a mission, however, it is very different. You are likely to be talking to a complete stranger after one of the mission events, perhaps a meal, a service or some event on neutral ground or in a home. Your graciousness and directness are likely to be particularly important.

Our attitude

Directness flies in the face of political correctness, which shuns confrontation, particularly in the area of politics or religion. But it is important, although widely neglected. After a talk it is not too difficult to ask someone what they thought of it, and whether they have reached the point in their lives yet where they have put their trust in Jesus Christ. It is easier if we refer back to when we took that step. But that gentle challenge can be just what the person needs. It helps them to take their own spiritual temperature. It often helps them to stop wavering on the edge, and decide.

Other qualities are also important. We must be natural, talking about response to God as easily as we talk about the meal we have just had. We must be in close touch with the Lord, trusting him to go ahead of us with his Holy Spirit, or we may make a mess of the whole conversation. We are going to need sensitivity, an intuition to know whether to pursue the questions or to draw back – because human pressure can be disastrous. We are going to need to pray as we speak, asking the Holy Spirit to convince the person of the truth of the gospel, show them their need of it, and encourage them to respond.

Opening the conversation

I will be making some suggestions about starting a conversation in a later chapter. When you meet someone after an evangelistic event introduce yourself and find out their name and something about them. Ask them about their impressions: 'Is this the first time you have been along to this Celebration? Was there anything that specially struck you this evening?' You will need to be guided by their response to that question, but I find it useful to have two diagnostic questions up my sleeve. The first goes something like this: 'Would you say that you have entrusted your life to Jesus Christ, or are you still thinking about it?' If the person says thankfully, 'I am still thinking about it,' that is a fair indication that he or she has not yet made a wholehearted response, and it is then easy for you to ask your second question, 'Would that be because there is something important you do not understand about the gospel, or is it, perhaps, that you are worried about what it might involve if you said yes?' Depending on their answer, you will be clear whether it is clarification that is needed, or gentle encouragement to take a step of faith.

Pointing the way

This will probably involve you summarising steps to faith, and seeing where the sticking point is. You will need to have some rough outline in your head, round which you build the verses of Scripture that have most helped you. It is valuable to use verses of Scripture, because it gives an objectivity to the whole proceeding. You are not just giving your own ideas, but pointing the person back to the basics of biblical faith. The words of the New Testament have a ring of truth about them that carries conviction more than any purely human explanations.

Handling the problems

When confronted with the loving call of Jesus Christ, people are often cut to the heart, and anxious to escape from radical challenge into more comfortable waters.

They may come up with one of the classic difficulties or excuses. There is a fundamental difference between the two. The difference is this: if you manage to dispose of a real difficulty then the person will quite easily come to Christ – the barrier has been removed. But if you knock down an excuse, he will tend to produce another excuse and thus keep you at arm's length. So the genuine difficulty needs to be handled with thoughtfulness and sensitivity, whereas the excuse needs to be exposed for the unworthy thing it is. You will need to pray for a lot of wisdom as you try to help at this juncture. Treat a difficulty as if it were a mere excuse and you will cause deep hurt. Spend a lot of time answering a problem that is only a smokescreen and you will get more smoke puffed in your face.

Some common excuses

'I have not got the time to go into it' is one such excuse. The answer is 'Yes, you have. In this respect everyone is equal. We all have exactly the same amount of time – and we use it to prioritise the things we think important. What you seem to mean is "I don't think Jesus is important."'

'There are so many hypocrites in the church' is another excuse that often comes up. Well, there are. Nobody pretends that the Christian church is flawless. But neither is your critic! So swallow down the temptation to say, 'Come along and make one more!' and maybe try to prick the bubble by asking him how many hypocrites he knows in the congregation and how he is so *sure* that they are hypocrites. Romans 4:12 is a valuable corrective to this excuse.

'I can be a Christian without going to church' is

another common get-out. There is a short answer to that one: Jesus couldn't (Luke 4:16)! But this whole attitude of doing the minimum is the very antithesis of someone who has genuinely been touched by the love of God and responded to it. Christianity is corporate, and it is generous. If 'being a Christian without . . .' is the attitude, he has missed the genuine article.

'I have always been a Christian' is a common response when someone is feeling the force of Christ's challenge. It is, of course, possible for someone born and raised in a loving and practising Christian home to grow up with the Lord in an ever deepening understanding and discipleship from earliest days. But generally when a person claims always to have been a Christian, take leave to doubt it! It is probable that either he is trying to pull wool over your eyes, or he is identifying being Christian with going to church (but see John 1:13, 2 Timothy 3:5), having been christened (but see Romans 2:28, Acts 8:13, 21), or doing his best (but see James 2:10, Matthew 22:37–39, Galatians 3:10). All these variations on the 'I've always been a Christian' theme are often excuses to conceal the fact that he has not yet surrendered to the love of Christ which is seeking him.

Excuses such as these, and there are plenty more, generally spring from a mixture of pride and prejudice. They are fed by fashion, laziness, ignorance, fear and materialism. These are the factors that help to confirm people in their genial undisclosed rebellion against God. It is our job gently to unmask them, and point to the truly amazing fact that God should continue to offer his pardon freely to those who are determined not to receive it (Romans 5:6–10).

Some common difficulties

There are a number of genuine difficulties and obstacles you will encounter as you try to help people to the point of commitment. Here are a few samples.

'*I really will make an effort to follow Christ.*' This is the sort of thing you will hear from time to time. That attitude, though praiseworthy in a way, springs from the Pelagianism that lies so deep within us: the misguided illusion that we have hearts of gold and that if only we polish them up a bit all will be well! We always want to *do* rather than receive. But the gospel is good news of what *God* has done for *us* – something to be embraced, not earned. It is not 'try' but 'trust' that lies at the heart of Christianity: not performance, but relationship. Much of the New Testament is devoted to making this plain: verses such as Romans 4:3–5 and Acts 16:31 point it up.

'*But I don't understand it all.*' some people will tell you – and this in the wake of your eloquent explanation! Of course they do not understand it all. How could any mortal fully take in what the almighty God has done to make us acceptable? '"What no eye has seen, nor ear heard, nor the heart of man conceived, what God has prepared for those who love him" God has revealed to us through the Spirit' (1 Corinthians 2:9–10). You do not need to understand electricity before you switch the light on, nor the nutrient value of food before you eat it. 'Taste and see that the Lord is good. Happy is the man who takes refuge in him' (Psalm 34:8). Your job is to encourage people to take a step of faith with as much understanding as they have. That is quite enough to establish contact. It is not so much rational understanding as personal commitment that starts relationship with Christ.

'*I have tried it all before, and it's no good*' is something that may come up. Try to find out what is the 'it' that he has tried. Is he confusing a deep turning to God with something less? Maybe he 'went forward' at a mission or crusade, but it never made any lasting difference. That could have been because his emotions were stirred but his will remained untouched. Or maybe his decision was real enough but he was never nurtured, never grew, and so gradually became indistinguishable from those who never began. Maybe he never took a public stand for Christ, or avoided getting linked up with the Christian community: he has shrivelled as a result. Maybe he never understood the power of the Holy Spirit in his life to break the grip of sinful habit. Perhaps the chill winds of his own doubts and the scepticism of others have withered the tiny shoot of faith.

You will need to exercise great care in handling this response. Show him that 'if we are faithless, he remains faithful – for he cannot deny himself' (2 Timothy 2:13); and so, if he genuinely yielded his will to Christ, Christ really has entered his life. Build from there. Show him that his state does not depend on his feelings but on the dependability of God, who has given us his word that 'he who has the Son has life; and he who does not have the Son of God does not have life' (1 John 5:12). Has he welcomed the Son into his life? If he has, however long ago and however tentatively, Christ has come in. Feed him with the promises of God. Let him learn some of them with you. It might be good to start with Revelation 3:20 and Matthew 28:20. Promises like these will prove an invaluable encouragement to the Christian who is making a new start. But if as he looks at his life he concludes that he has never really begun the path of discipleship in earnest, then lead him to it as you would anyone else.

'*I am not sure if I am a Christian or not.*' When faced by someone like this it is a mistake to urge them to make a further decision. That can be quite destructive to an indecisive person. Rather stress the promises of God if we come to him (John 6:37, Romans 8:1, Ephesians 2:1). Point to the cross (Hebrews 10:10–14). Christ's work there is more than sufficient for the needs of the whole world and never needs to be repeated or supplemented. Bills do not need to be paid twice! And encourage him to look for the signs of the new life in Christ. We are meant to know where we stand, not to hope in uncertainty and fear. Indeed, the whole First Letter of John is designed to meet this quest for assurance, and I will be looking at it in the next chapter, as we reflect on the nurture of new Christians.

Sometimes a thoughtful person will say wistfully, '*I could never keep it up.*' He is quite right. None of us can. The whole point is that Christ will keep him up once he comes into the life. Promises such as 1 Peter 1:5, John 10:28f and Jude 24 make that very plain. Once again we are driven back to the unfamiliar but absolutely necessary path of trust. It is Christ's job to keep me from falling, but it is mine to trust him to do so.

'*A friend said I am not a proper Christian because I have not been baptised in the Holy Spirit*' is a stumbling-block one may occasionally meet. Certain churches are very dogmatic in asserting that unless you speak in tongues you are not a real Christian; or conversely, if you do, that you must be acting under psychological or even demonic influence. Because of this polarisation (some churches even asserting that such gifts died out in the second century) it is unwise to get too involved in a debate on the topic unless the person is keen to follow it through. One helpful thing to remember is that while we

are enjoined to be filled with the Spirit (Ephesians 5:18 –
a present continuous tense is used: it is not a once-for-all
experience), nowhere in the New Testament is the phrase
'baptism in the Holy Spirit' used of a second stage in
Christian initiation. All its seven references are concerned
with the initial entry into the realm of the Spirit when we
become Christians (Matthew 3:11, Mark 1:8, Luke 3:16,
John 1:33, Acts 1:5, 11:16, 1 Corinthians 12:13). There
is no suggestion in the New Testament that there are two
sorts of Christians – those who have been baptised with
the Spirit and those who have not. On the contrary, 'If
anyone does not have the Spirit of Christ he is not a
Christian' (see Romans 8:9) is the clear teaching of the
Bible. We need to encourage the person to go deeper in
the life of the Spirit, to ask the Spirit to endow them with
any gifts they need for Christ's service, and to cultivate
the fruit of the Spirit.

There are of course many major difficulties like other
faiths and the problem of evil and suffering which cannot
be treated here, and rarely come up when you reach the
point of decision. At that point perhaps the most
common of all difficulties is fear.

'*I'm afraid*' is an honest difficulty, and not at all
surprising. Help her to analyse that fear. Is she afraid that
nothing might happen? If so, take her back to the
promise of Jesus, 'I *will* come in.' Jesus can be trusted not
to break his word. Is she afraid that she will be letting
herself in for a life of misery or tedium? Far from it. 'In
your presence there is fulness of joy: in your right hand
are pleasures for evermore', as the psalmist knew (Psalm
16:11). Is she scared of being in a minority? She will be,
but then one plus Christ is always a majority. Anyway,
since when has the majority always been right? Is she
afraid of what her friends would say? That is the usual

problem. Show her that any friends who are worthwhile will not desert her. Show her that she is not called to become a religious prig. Show her that she is not required to drop her friends – simply to be among them as before but with Jesus just beneath the surface of her life. Show her that perfect love will cast out these fears of hers (1 John 4:18) and that she is about to welcome the perfect love of God into her life.

The step of faith

The time has come when things seem pretty clear and the flow of questions has dried up a bit. Ask gently, 'Do you think you are ready to say "Yes" to the Lord now? Or is there anything that is still keeping you back from him?' If he can't think of anything, say, 'Right, then let's kneel down right away and ask him to come into your life' (or whatever analogy you are using). Alternatively you can ask him if he would prefer to make that solemn act of commitment on his own, and tell you when he has done so. Or would he like your presence and support at this important time? Most people, you will find, opt for your help.

If so, sit or kneel close to him and then encourage him to pray for himself. The prayer may be short: 'God be merciful to me a sinner' was, Jesus told us, sufficient to send a man down to his house 'justified' (Luke 18:13–14). He may well want to build on the promise of Revelation 3:20 and ask the Spirit of the long excluded Jesus Christ to come into his life. He may, as in Luke 11:13, ask the Father to give the Holy Spirit to him. It is not so much the content of the prayer as the reality of the commitment that matters. But it is important to encourage him, in any case, to ask the Lord to clean up his past life and put his Holy Spirit within.

It matters little whether he prays out loud (which he will probably never have done in his life) or silently. If he prefers the silent option ask him to give you some indication of when he has finished. You can then praise God for and with him. But it is often good to encourage him to pray aloud. Tell him, 'This doesn't mean that God can't hear you if you pray silently, but I think it will help to seal the commitment if you do it out loud.' Then he will usually do so with few inhibitions, and often with great freedom and joy.

In either case, it is an enormous privilege to be alongside someone at a time like this. It often moves me to tears. And then I pray that the Holy Spirit will baptise the person deeply into Christ, lavish spiritual gifts upon them, and never leave them. It is generally a time of some emotions: tears and laughter often mingle in both of you. But it is important, in the sheer joy of the moment, not to omit vital things that need immediate attention before you leave each other.

The immediate sequel

1. He needs to be clear where he stands

I generally turn to my friend and ask, 'Did Jesus put his Spirit in your heart when you asked him?' In most cases he knows the answer without a shadow of doubt. But not always. In which case, I take him back to the promise of Christ: 'He says, "If anyone opens the door I will come in." Did you open the door?'

'Well yes, as best I know how.'

'Then he has come in. He does not break his word. You see, faith means trusting the faithfulness of God, not your own volatile feelings. Jesus promised that he would come in – not that you would immediately feel different!'

And then I do with him what I would do with anyone who is already sure. I encourage him to thank God for what has happened.

2. He needs to express his gratitude

He does not want to be like an ungrateful child, slow to give thanks for a birthday present. So encourage the spirit of thankfulness in him from the start. Ask him to thank the Lord for coming in. And this time there is hardly ever any problem about praying aloud, 'Dear Lord, thank you so much for entering my life. Thank you for your promise that you will not leave me. Help me to be true to you all my days.' A prayer like that is an early lesson. He needs to come to God with gratitude and praise, not just with requests.

3. He needs initial protection against doubt

Doubts always crowd in after someone has made a commitment to Christ. Was it real? Was I just an emotional fool? Will it last? What happens when I do something wrong? You would be wise not to attempt anything comprehensive at this stage, but it would be good to send him away with a single promise of Christ in his mind to counteract doubt. I often use 1 John 5:11–12: 'He who has the Son has life, and he who does not have the Son of God does not have life.' Does he 'have' the Son? Why, yes if he has invited him to share his life. Then he has God's life, God's eternal life, in him. I get him to repeat the promise and its reference several times, and maybe mark it in a New Testament that I give him. Warn him that doubt is Satan's prime weapon against the new believer. If the devil cannot stop someone becoming a Christian he will do his best to ensure that he does not enjoy it and is not sure about it! And the sooner the new

Christian learns, like his Master, to face doubts with the promises of Scripture and say, 'It is written,' the sooner he will find his feet as a Christian and grow.

4. *He needs to tell someone else*

The New Testament insists in a variety of ways that we need to confess with our mouth that we belong to Jesus, and not merely believe in him secretly in our hearts. Show him that very point in Romans 10:9–10. He will find it difficult initially, but an enormous help in the long run, to go and tell someone else that the commitment has been made. Encourage him to make a start by finding someone who will be glad to hear it! He may be aware of a friend or relative who has been praying for him for some time. What a joy it will be for that person when he goes and tells them. If the new believer is a youngster living at home he might be wise to let his life speak for a while before trying to say anything to his parents (and getting put down). If he or she has come to Christ from another faith, particularly Islam, Judaism or Hinduism, there is sure to be massive opposition. Christians are still persecuted in many countries, even to death. It would be wise to allow his life to speak for a considerable period until he has built up enough resources to face the consequences of a public profession of faith. But, given that proviso, a new Christian needs to tell someone else reasonably soon, for it will greatly strengthen his own spiritual life when he does so.

5. *He needs tender loving care*

Very soon the enemy will be at work, seeking to destroy a fledgling Christian life. So you too must be at work, helping him to see what strength and riches he has inherited in Christ. He has had quite enough for one day, but arrange to meet him in a day or two when you can help him in the early problems he will encounter and show him how to grow in the life of discipleship. Meanwhile give him a booklet like John Stott's *Becoming a Christian*, Nicky Gumbel's *Why Jesus?* or my *Come, Follow Me*. He can take it away, read it at leisure, and reflect on the magnitude of what has happened as he enters on the most exciting of all relationships, with Jesus Christ as his Saviour and Lord. And don't forget to complete the response card if the mission is using them. Then you will not have to trust your fallible memory for his name, address, phone number, and when you agreed to meet him next!

7

Nurture – How dare we neglect it?

If the title of this chapter seems a little aggressive, that is because I feel very strongly about it. It is little less than criminal to bring someone to the step of commitment to Jesus Christ, and then to leave them to get on with it. And yet that happens time after time in evangelistic missions and crusades. All the emphasis is on getting people to hear the gospel and urging them to respond to it, and little care is taken over the sequel. But a moment's reflection will show that the new believer may well be as weak and defenceless spiritually as a new-born baby is in the physical realm.

As our society becomes more and more unchurched and profoundly ignorant of Christian teaching, resources and lifestyle, it is more essential than ever to concentrate on building up in the faith those who have come to God through Christ. They have entered a new world, and they need to learn its ways. The first Christians gave enormous care to this nurture of believers, but today it has become a very neglected area, and we are paying the price not only through those who fall away but through those untaught Christians who limp along with a lifestyle that is indistinguishable from the secular society from which they came, and with no idea on how to help anyone else to faith.

It is obvious, then, that people need a lot of help at this watershed of their lives, when they have entrusted themselves to Christ but are probably confused about what they have done and unclear about what it will involve to live as Christians in a world that does not acknowledge God. They need information. They need encouragement. They need to be drawn into the Christian community. They need help in developing a devotional life. They need to get into the habit of worshipping. They need to learn the reasons for the hope they cherish. They need to be nourished by the Word and the sacraments. They need someone to look after them and help with their initial doubts and questions. They need examples of Christian lives to emulate. They need above all to be loved.

So I would like to suggest two approaches which I have found very helpful in a wide variety of circumstances. The first we shall look at in this chapter. It concerns the precedents we find for nurture in the New Testament itself. The second, which I will address in the following chapter, concerns a wonderfully practical way of helping people to grow, the nurture group.

The New Testament has a lot to teach us on the topic. Indeed, we find it was a major concern on the birthday of the church, the Day of Pentecost itself. There seem to have been seven main aspects to their nurture of converts.

Baptism

Those who believed, we are told, were baptised, 'and there were added to the church about three thousand souls' (Acts 2:41). Repentance and faith was not enough.

They needed to undergo the rite of baptism which Jesus had inaugurated (Matthew 28:19). Interestingly, the apostles did not require a long catechumenate before they baptised them. They did it at once. And why not? Should not the new Christian have the badge of Christian belonging? To be sure, it is risky. But they did it because they saw repentance, faith, baptism and the reception of the Holy Spirit as very much four aspects of one thing: incorporation into Christ. Indeed, so closely did the New Testament writers construe this link that they sometimes spoke in instrumental terms about baptism: 'as many of you as were baptised into Christ have put on Christ' or 'baptism now saves you' (Galatians 3:27 and 1 Peter 3:21). They saw baptism as the sign and seal on the new life in Christ, and the means whereby it became obvious to others, and brought assurance to the recipient. New believers need to be baptised.

If they have already been baptised, perhaps in infancy as is the practice in many churches, most Christians would agree that they do not need to be baptised again. Baptism is the sacrament of Christian beginnings, and is, by definition, unrepeatable. Of course, some people do repeat it, but that makes no more sense than getting married to the same person several times, or getting adopted into the same family again and again! Baptism is the mark of the start of following Christ, just as Communion is the mark of continuing with him. Thus one sacrament is unrepeatable, and the other frequently repeated. What, then, are we to do if our new believer has already been baptised? Well, baptism does not need to be repeated, but he or she does need the opportunity to confess Christ publicly. That is the confessional aspect of baptism which such folk have, by definition, been unable to take part in, because they have hitherto had no living

faith to profess. Opportunity needs to be given for them
to give testimony in a main service, as this is not only a
great blessing in their own lives but an enormous encouragement to the congregation, and a reminder that the
gospel continues to have power to save.

Teaching

The first converts, we are told, continued 'in the apostles'
teaching' (Acts 2:42). What was it?

First and foremost it must have been teaching about
Jesus, the sort of material we find recorded in the
Gospels. Who was this Jesus they had come to trust?
What did he teach? Why was he killed? Could they be
sure that he had beaten the powers of death? Those were
some of the questions that would have sprung to the
minds of new believers. They still do. They demand an
answer.

Second, it seems to have been teaching about fulfilment. That was where Jesus began (Mark 1:15). That
was where Peter's address at Pentecost began: 'This is
what was spoken by the prophet Joel' (Acts 2:16). By
'this' he meant the fulfilment of the Old Testament
prophecy embodied in the gift of tongues, the radiant joy
on the streets, the evident sense of newness and discovery.
Healing and prophetic gifts were to follow, along with
fearless and unquenchable evangelism. All the strands of
truth in Judaism, and indeed in the best of pagan
thought, had reached their culmination in the man of
Nazareth, whom God had made both Messiah and Lord.
In that confidence of fulfilment they could confront the
Jews and Gentiles alike. They did not need to surrender
to the syncretism and pluralism all around them. They
had been discovered and set free by nothing less than

Truth incarnate. This sense of fulfilment in Christ is an important element in the spiritual growth of new Christians.

Third, this teaching consisted of a short and brilliant sequence of ethical instruction, which probably followed baptism and was widely used in the early church. We find traces of it in James, Hebrews and 1 Peter, but it is never more clearly laid out than by the apostle Paul in Colossians and Ephesians. There we find the following injunctions, and in much the same order. Put off the old nature, put on the new (Colossians 3:9f, Ephesians 4:22–24); submit (Colossians 3:18, Ephesians 5:22); watch and pray (Colossians 4:2, Ephesians 6:18); and stand (Colossians 4:12, Ephesians 6:11). Note the similarities to this teaching of Paul in 1 Peter (2:1, 2:4–9, 2:13ff, 4:7 and 5:8f). It is much the same in James (1:21, 4:7, 5:16). In both 1 Peter and James this follows reference to the believer's new birth (1 Peter 1:23, James 1:18). The variety of New Testament teachers who use this material suggests that it was standard teaching for new believers, and what a magnificent teaching course this material makes! This is how it might be developed.

1. A session on the new birth, and the radical transformation it will bring with it. The convert will need to be clear about this, or he will build on a shaky foundation.

2. An examination and discussion of some of the things from the old life which will have to go.

3. A lesson on the image of God in which mankind was made. It was lost through human disobedience, restored in the person of Jesus and gradually imparted to the believer by the Spirit as he transforms us into the likeness

of Christ. The new life needs to be put on deliberately, daily, like a suit of new clothes.

4. Christians are not called to throw their weight about, but to live in submission to their Lord and to each other. The husband must as much submit to his wife in loving care and protection as she must to him as the leader of the family. And the same applies in our relationships with one another. Jesus lived the life of the Servant, and so must we.

5. New Christians need to learn how to 'stand', or to 'withstand' the evil one. The devil is real, and must be resisted in the new-found power of Jesus Christ. Discipleship does not mean a sudden burst of enthusiasm but a long-term standing up for Jesus.

6. They need to learn how to watch and pray. It is interesting that these two generally come together. Unless they watch they will not pray: the prayer time will get squeezed out. And unless they watch in another sense, they will not go on praying. For they will not notice the answers to their prayers, and will become discouraged.

Finally, the importance of the Word of God and love for one another were stressed by all three New Testament writers (see above). Such seems to have been the basic ethical teaching for converts, and it was complemented in many instances, we may imagine, by the warnings against false teaching which are common to 2 Peter and Jude.

Fellowship

The earliest Christians 'continued in the apostles' fellowship' (Acts 2:42). That fellowship was very warm. They shared their possessions, they sold property to meet one another's needs, and their love and unity astonished the ancient world. Their fellowship took three forms, all of them highly relevant today.

First, there was the personal attention that we all crave, especially upon moving into a new situation. And the new Christian has certainly done just that, and needs a lot of personal care at this stage of his development. I recall the regular one-to-one meetings with Richard Gorrie, who brought me to faith. He gave me so much encouragement, showed me how to read and feed on the Scriptures, and patiently helped me with my doubts and difficulties. I owe him more than I can say. I doubt if I would have been a practising Christian today without his care all those years ago. Where would Timothy have been without Paul? And where would Paul himself have been without Ananias or Barnabas? People need that pastoral care, and all too often do not get it. If each new Christian had a time of prayer, Bible reading, companionship and problem-sharing with a more mature believer once a week for a couple of months, growth would be solid. That is not theory. Experience is speaking!

Second, alongside personal attention there needs to be the fellowship of a small group of caring, relaxed fellow Christians. The first believers met in homes, and that has much to commend it. The informal atmosphere, the food and laughter all make it easy to move into spiritual issues, and help the new Christians to adjust to the new society they have joined. It is no accident that the churches which are growing fastest worldwide are usually those which meet in small cells, and multiply by drawing other friends in. Other lively churches split their congregations down into home fellowship groups. In either case, it is the warm informal fellowship of the small group that is such a help in the early days of discipleship.

A third area of fellowship is, of course, the church congregation. New believers need to be introduced gradually, and in a way that does not embarrass them. Never forget that church culture is so different from the rest of society that it is quite a shock for a newcomer. In a large church it helps to have a Welcome Desk which has up-to-date information on the various fellowship groups, nursery arrangements, sectional interests, and forthcoming congregational special events. It is a valuable way to help people to integrate into the appropriate part of the life of the church.

In these three ways, the new believer will become accustomed to and greatly benefit from that wonderful means of God's grace, Christian fellowship.

Worship

The earliest Christians took part in what Luke calls 'the breaking of bread' (Acts 2:42), doubtless the Holy Communion. This is what Jesus had commanded, and it became the characteristic form of Christian worship. New believers need to be brought speedily into the eucharistic fellowship of the church. We are physical beings, and much about Christianity seems to be 'spiritual' and hard to get a grip on. But eating is the most basic human activity; maybe that is one reason why Jesus chose it for us to remember him by and meet him in. It is a meal of deepest profundity which we will never exhaust. But the new believer can begin right away. He can easily understand that the broken bread represents the body of Jesus broken for him on the cross, the poured-out wine his spilled blood. And his heart will be warmed in gratitude. He can easily understand that just as the bread and wine nourish his body, so Jesus, the bread and wine of life, nourishes his soul. Just as he takes the bread and wine into himself and makes it part of him, so he feeds on Christ, takes him deep within his being, and makes him part of his own life. Nor is it too difficult to understand that the Communion is a foretaste of the final banquet in heaven, presided over by the Father, and with all his family present.

Naturally the Communion is not the only form of worship the church offers. Just as in Judaism the synagogue service of the Word balanced the sacramental worship in the temple feasts, so it should be in the church. There should be non-sacramental services full of joy, the opportunity for testimony, awe and wonder as worship becomes not a duty but a joy. Worship should actually comprise one half of the work of the church on earth; the other half is mission in its broadest sense. Worship of God and ministry to humankind are the two supreme callings of the church, and the new believer needs to find his place in them. Many, of course, will already be used to church worship. It may have been one of the main factors in bringing them to Christ.

Prayer

Prayer is somewhat foreign to most people. They may pray in a crisis. They may even pray more than they would ever care to admit. But it is not as natural to them as breathing. It is not yet a way of life. And one of the initial changes that accompanies the new relationship with Christ is that prayer does become natural. The Spirit within the new Christian teaches him to address the Father with the intimacy proper to members of the family, 'Abba, dear Father' (Romans 8:15). But prayer will need a great deal of encouraging: personal prayer, prayer in a group, prayer at odd moments of the day as he learns to look up into the Lord's face. Many people have found the acronym ACTS helpful in the early days of their discipleship: Adoration, Confession, Thanksgiving and Supplication. And that will in due course develop into imaginative prayer, taking an incident in the gospel and mulling it over prayerfully. It will lead deeper into contemplative prayer when we do not ask for anything but simply revel in the presence of the beloved Lord. But start with short extemporary prayers expressing repentance, thanksgiving and requests. Learn from some of the first words a child acquires: sorry, thank you and please! But the new Christian will want a lot of help along the way, not least in the area of unanswered prayer. A regular prayer breakfast or small prayer group will be the best climate in which such problems can be resolved. By sheer practice he needs to discover that prayer is as vital as breathing.

Witness and service

One of the most striking differences between the early Christians and those in mainline churches these days is that in the first century new Christians were giving testimony very early on and soon got involved in the work of the Christian community. They saw themselves as limbs in the body of Christ. Everyone had a job to do, and everyone had a responsibility to stand up and be counted as a Christian. This witness was not self-advertisement. It was testimony to the fact that Jesus Christ is alive and highly relevant.

In many Third World countries this is the norm. There

is massive lay witness to Christ. In the West we are crippled with embarrassment even to mention the name of Jesus. Until we get over that, the church will not grow. New Christians are very good at witnessing, if they are given a little encouragement. They are so artless and unaffected. They have made a life-changing discovery. They are uninhibited. Moreover they have many friends who are not Christians. So they are often the best evangelists. And it is important to harness their enthusiasm into cheerful testimony and practical service. We do not take enough risks with new believers. We mistakenly think they cannot do anything until they know more. This is foolish. There are always more tasks for the Christian community to fulfil than there are enough hands to do them, so why not encourage new converts to try? My wife was leading a Bible study (very badly, she would tell you) within a few weeks of professing faith as a new student at Oxford. Recently I had a 25-year-old to dinner who is a dynamic and, by now, very experienced leader. This is largely due to the careful training she received from her vicar in Christian doctrine and church history when she was a raw new convert at university. Three hours a week! She tells me that twelve lay assistants emerged from that vicar's little group, most of whom are now on the way to ordination. Witness and service are two vital elements in Christian growth.

Oversight

Another feature which was constant in the pattern of nurture to be found in the New Testament is pastoral oversight. The new convert had someone to look after him in the early days. Mark had his Peter, Silvanus his Paul. In our egalitarian society we are sometimes suspicious of oversight. But it is very important. In the New Testament we find the leadership setting an example, exercising discipline, taking young Christians on missionary journeys, encouraging them and writing letters. All of this is needed today if we are to mould new disciples.

A moment's thought will show us how much help the new believer needs. First, he needs immediate help over doubt. Who has not asked himself, in the aftermath of encounter with Christ, whether or not it was real or simply a flash of emotion? This doubt needs to be handled, or it will fester.

When initial doubt has been dealt with, and Christian assurance seen to depend in the first instance on the promise of God, the cross of Christ and the promised presence of the Spirit, there will be other urgent matters that need attention. The new believer will, as we have seen, need tactful and appropriate introduction to the church. He will need help in developing a devotional life. It would be good to introduce him to the notes provided by the Scripture Union or Bible Reading Fellowship, which suggest a short passage for daily reading with helpful explanatory notes and application to life.

Then there will certainly be ethical issues that sooner or later need to be addressed. There will be a host of problems – some intellectual, some moral, some sexual, some financial – which need help from a wise Christian friend who has been a disciple of Christ for some time. The most natural person to fulfil such a role is the one who has led the new believer into the faith. This may, of course, not be possible. But in any case some loving Christian who is relaxed, relational and unshockable is needed, who can be a model, a friend and a leader for the new believer. But when there are a number of new converts it may become difficult to find enough mature people who have the skills and time to look after them one on one. So over the years I have come to the conclusion that one of the most helpful things is for the new believer to join a group under competent leadership where all the members are new Christians or are contemplating starting the Christian life. Such groups provide a marvellous launching pad for discipleship, and I want to say more about them in the next chapter.

8

The Nurture Group –
How could we run it?

The idea

The idea of the nurture group is very simple. It is nothing
more than a number of new or fairly new Christians (and
maybe some not quite decided yet) meeting together for
study, prayer and companionship under the leadership of
two or three experienced Christians, ideally lay people.
Despite not being a layman I have had the joy of running
such groups for many years. They are a marvellous way
of helping new Christians to grow. They are valuable
teaching tools, great fun, and build relationships which
overflow in dynamic life for the church.

The value of such groups is not hard to appreciate. For
one thing, the use of a nurture group ensures that competent people are looking after the development of new
Christians; people who have responsibility both towards
those in their group and towards the church which has
entrusted them with the task. For another, it teaches the
new Christians the joy and the importance of fellowship,
perhaps before they have even heard it explained. Moreover, it incorporates the one-to-one care referred to in the

previous chapter, which is so important in the early days of discipleship. But it transposes it into a different key because of the group dimension. Each of the leaders will make himself personally responsible for taking time with and discipling two or three members of the group, so that every one of them has a personal mentor. Naturally these personal sessions take place outside the group meeting time. So the new believer gets his or her personal attention, but is also greatly enriched by what goes on in the group. For it is here that they can share their fears and discoveries. It is here that they can grow and see others grow. They can listen to others' stories of answered prayer and relate their own experiences. They can raise problems, and listen to the answers, as others voice difficulties they feel but have not articulated. Another great advantage of such a group is that it leads naturally into the network of home fellowship groups which are such a healthy dimension in most growing churches but are not particularly suited for raw new disciples, until they have found their sea legs, so to speak. And that is precisely what the nurture group enables them to do.

The aim of the group is clear. It is to 'present everyone mature in Christ Jesus' (Colossians 1:28) so far as that is practicable within a period of eight to ten weeks, the optimum time for such a course. Mature enough, at least, to know he or she is a Christian disciple, and to begin to be able to give an account of why. Mature enough to have a regular devotional life, and to have told someone else that she is a Christian. Mature enough to know what the church is about, and to be able to take his place within the fellowship. Mature enough to want to start serving the Lord in some way or other. That is what one might expect to come out of a nurture group, and it very often does. My experience suggests that only a tiny proportion of those who profess the faith fall away if they are incorporated into one of these courses. It seems to provide a foundation for their Christian lives. It is the best way I know of following up those who come to faith as adults.

The numbers involved should be large enough to form a viable group even if one or two are away for some reason, but small enough to ensure that there are no passengers in the group – everyone gets involved. The ratio of leaders to members is important. Mostly the leaders will have regular secular jobs and cannot realistically take personal care of more than two or at most three members during the life of the course. So you would need four leaders for a large group of ten or twelve.

The members of the group may well be very diverse. I have had groups with doctoral students sitting alongside unemployed alcoholics, and it works. After all, in the Christian family we do not choose our brothers and sisters. Variety is, in fact, an asset in the group. And they will assuredly be at different stages spiritually. Some will be there for a refresher course. Some will have very recently put their trust in Christ, and others will be thinking about it. Sometimes people have no idea why they are there: they signed up under some impulse of the Spirit of God, but they cannot explain it and are probably embarrassed! The first meeting, if skilfully led, should handle that.

The meeting

I was privileged to work in a large church where we saw many conversions, and so we devised a course which followed a clear plan. There was welcoming coffee as people arrived, and then we settled down for an hour and a half to make good use of the evening. There was always an overriding theme for each occasion, but a number of elements fed into that single theme. One of the leaders gave a short talk on the subject, followed by group discussion. We all learned a verse of Scripture by heart, on the same subject. Then, if it was a large group, we would split into two sub-groups and do an inductive Bible study on the same subject as the preceding talk, with all the members sharing their insights from the passage. That would lead naturally into prayers from the group members. Often a few carefully chosen books on the theme of the evening would be available for borrowing or purchase. At the end of the evening we would give each person a sheet of notes which would serve as a concise summary of what had taken place. These sheets enabled members to go back over the evening's teaching, check the Scripture verses, and by the end of the course they would have a sketchy, but not inconsiderable, series of flysheets on a number of basic doctrines.

Our topics began with Beginning as a Christian, then Christian Assurance, Reading the Bible, Learning to Pray, the Holy Spirit, Christian Fellowship, Defeating Evil, and Serving Christ. The order was deliberate. The first evening gave the opportunity to explain that real Christianity is a relationship with Christ, and how to enter it. It was often a very significant time for people to commit themselves not just to the course but to Christ. You cannot build a good house on a rotten foundation, so it was important next for members to enter into a deep assurance that they belonged to God's family. The relationship needs to be nurtured through regular exposure to the milk and gradually the strong meat of the Word of God, so it was vital to find out how to read the Scriptures devotionally and feed on them. Prayer is the Christian's lifeblood, and yet little is generally taught about it.

We were keen for members to see the importance of prayer, fulfil the conditions of answered prayer and experience the joy of it, both individually and with others. An evening on the Holy Spirit enables you not only to teach about the person and work of the Spirit, but to challenge people to be filled with the Spirit and to welcome his gifts and power. This was often a crucial evening for commitment and re-commitment among members of the group. A major session on the church, its membership, fellowship and sacraments occupied a further evening. It is important for Christians not to live lives that are continually defeated, and so an evening on the way to victorious living was clearly necessary. And finally, we had a concluding evening on serving Christ and being not just a Christian consumer but a Christian commando. At this stage the group disbanded, and members were allotted to one of the regular home groups.

The choice of passages of Scripture we studied was not crucial. For example on the first evening, when the aim was to give clarity about Christian commitment, one could choose between John 3:1–16, Luke 19:1–10 or Acts 9:1–19. All three speak of the life-transforming encounter with Jesus Christ that we long for all members of the group to experience. The verse to learn for the evening could be John 3:16, Revelation 3:20 or Matthew 11:28. All teach the same truth. There was no crippling uniformity in the way different groups were run. The themes were basic, but the way they were handled varied from group to group.

Often it was found helpful to give a short talk on the topic to start with, so that people could be very clear on the direction of the evening and have a chance to raise objections and difficulties.

No less valuable was the inductive Bible study to reinforce the theme of the evening, and to teach the members to draw thoughts out of Scripture and make them their own. The skill for the leader lay in saying as little as possible but asking shrewd questions which got everyone else contributing. It was a very exciting part of the evening to see members who were quite unused to the Bible begin to wrestle with its meaning, and get excited as they found how it spoke to their situation.

Another element which proved invaluable was learning a verse of Scripture by heart. We got them to repeat, and so learn, a verse, with its reference, which encapsulated the theme of the evening. Hiding portions of Scripture away in the heart is done all too little these days, and the proliferation of Bible translations does not make it any easier, but if new Christians learn a verse a week for eight weeks they have started a very good habit and are soon able to help other people.

A further element which contributes to growth is to mention one or two suitable books which the leaders will have brought with them for sale or loan. It does not matter so much what the books are, so long as they are relevant to the theme and readable. The value lies in getting people reading and therefore thinking intelligently about their faith. Often, too, some of the deeper questions which emerge during an evening are best dealt with by lending the questioner a book and not by involving everyone else in an extended discussion which may be irrelevant to their needs.

The last part of the evening will be prayer, perhaps in silence, but more often extempore so that all can agree with the sentiment expressed, and say their amen, 'so be it!'. It will help people in the group if they are encouraged to take one phrase of the Bible passage they have been studying together and turn it into a one-sentence prayer.

In this way people are more likely to break the sound barrier. This praying in of thoughts which emerge from Scripture is, of course, good modelling for what we hope will become the disciple's own time of daily prayer and Bible reading.

The evening will end after prayer, but generally people have had such a good time that they are in no hurry to run away, and it is an excellent time to chat, arrange one-on-one sessions, and talk further, if need be, about problems that have emerged. Alternatively it may simply be a time of chilling out and relaxing.

Leading a nurture group

How do you find leaders for such a group? The best ones are those with natural people skills, able to make others feel at ease and loved. Their friendliness, tact, unshockability and good humour is much more important than massive Bible knowledge. It helps if at least one among the leadership is a person who has led groups before and is well instructed, but assistant leaders often emerge from those who have recently been through the course themselves. They understand from recent experience what it is to come to Christian faith from a very different way of life, and so they easily relate to enquirers and people who are struggling to get started. I look for people who are teachable rather than academic; apprenticeship is the best way to learn.

Leaders need to know and trust each other and have an easy working relationship. So it is good to meet for a meal and share the story of each other's spiritual pilgrimage before the group meets at all. This will also enable you to find out each other's interests, strengths, experience, likes and dislikes. Time invested in this way is never wasted. It will pay off handsomely in the running of the group. The bonding of the leaders provides an attractive model for the members to notice and emulate.

When the course gets under way, the leaders will meet beforehand to pray and make sure coffee and a welcome are prepared. They will stay on at the end to review how the evening went, learn any lessons, and share out the work for the next week, deciding who will get the books, make the coffee, arrange the room, do the inductive Bible reading, teach the verse and give the short talk. They will have noticed if anyone was missing, and will call round some time in the following days to take the notes of the evening session and say how much the absentee was missed. Such signs of care and interest almost invariably mean the person will not miss the meeting again.

All in all, the quality of relationships between the leaders will almost certainly determine the feel and the growing intimacy of the group. If there is tension or jealousy among them, it will immediately be spotted by members of the group. Mutual love, example and naturalness in handling questions will all have a silent eloquence.

There are several sides to the leadership of such groups.

Leadership on the first evening

This is absolutely crucial. This is when you win them or lose them. The most experienced leader should handle it. Naturally people will feel on edge when they come, not knowing what to expect. After all, they are not used to talking about God in a private house on a weekday evening. So the leadership team needs to welcome everyone with a smile and a drink as they come in, and then move around chatting and helping people to relax. After about ten minutes, ask people to grab a chair and gather round in a circle (so that you can have eye contact with everyone). A good way to start is to say, 'It would be good if we could all say a bit about ourselves, what brings us here, and what we hope to get out of it.' Then kick off yourself with, 'Maybe I'd better begin . . .' Say a little about yourself and your situation, and succinctly explain how you came to a living faith in Christ. Then pass to another of your leaders, sitting next to you, and ask her to tell a bit of her story and how she came to faith.

This will set the scene for others to follow, and you will be intrigued to hear stories, some of them astonishing, of the work of God in bringing people to the house that evening. Some of them will be Christians. Some will not be sure what they are. Some will be on the brink of decision. Others will have serious obstacles to faith. You need to make everyone comfortable about what they have said, and some deft comments by you as leader can facilitate this and make them feel it is OK to be an agnostic, or whatever, at this stage. Make it plain that you will not be doing this again, lest they get the wrong idea of how these evenings will proceed. But it is such a good thing to do on the first night. You will have gained a lot through this simple exercise. Everyone will have given some sort of spiritual testimony as to where they stand with God. Each of them will have trusted the other members of the group with that information. And as a result they will have broken the ice and will from now on be able to talk about quite personal spiritual things with those who earlier in the evening were complete strangers to them. All this can lead very naturally into the short talk about what real Christianity is, and the evening can take its planned course.

Leadership in the short talk

The talk at the start of each evening is a real challenge. It has to be intriguing. It must not sound like a sermon. It must welcome interruptions. It needs to be short and crystal clear. It aims to get the Bible open in front of them so that they can see that this book packs power. Your biggest dangers will be to go on too long, or to assume they know too much. Do not imagine they will bring a Bible the first night. You must have some ready to lend them (as well as some to sell if you have a bookstall). And you would be wise to have them all the same version, or you will waste endless time responding to querulous and unprofitable complaints: 'Oh, my version does not say that. It says . . .' These may be small points, but careful preparation and gracious leadership are needed. If you take trouble over the details, the evening will flow. And so great is the ignorance these days that you may well need to say, as they open the Bible at the wrong end, 'There are two parts to this book, the Old Testament and the New Testament. We'll look into this more later on, but for now let's turn to page . . . of the New Testament.'

If you manage on that first evening to get across to the group the essence of what Christian commitment means, and help them to see there is a definite choice to be made, you will have done well. There may not be time to do an inductive Bible study the first night, depending on how long the introductions have taken. But it is good to do one if you can, for it begins to cut their teeth on using the Bible for themselves and sensing its relevance. It will also be a good launch pad for their own personal Bible reading if they have not got round to that yet.

Leadership in the inductive Bible study

This can be tricky, and it calls for relaxed and yet very intentional leadership. If you have a big group, split it into two for this part of the evening, with at least one leader in each. These Bible studies are not so much a teaching exercise as a voyage of discovery on the theme of the evening. As leader you are there to stimulate, to referee and to encourage. You are not there to dominate, and certainly not to preach. Lead from behind. Trust the Holy Spirit to teach your folk. Allow members to make mistakes without jumping on them. Initially it does not matter much what they say so long as they say something and get used to the sound of their own voice talking about God and the Bible.

Gather the small group round, with Bibles open at the right place. Offer a brief prayer to God for insight and understanding. Then get the members to read round, a verse or two each. (Be sensitive though to any who are dyslexic or have difficulty reading.) Then say, 'We are going to have two whole minutes of complete quiet now, so that we can read it through again to ourselves, and see what most strikes us. Then we will pool those thoughts and learn from one another.'

Your heart may miss a beat waiting for someone to start after the two minutes are up, but somebody will. And then you are away. It may be hard to stop them by the end of the study. It is good getting people to mention what verse they are finding helpful. This both concentrates their own ideas, and enables others to concentrate on the same thing. Two big things to avoid are red herrings and cross-references to other parts of Scripture. If you allow people to chase after a cross-reference you have lost them irretrievably. If you allow 'red herring fishing' you might all just as well pack up and go home. Everyone will air their own ideas on matters about which they know next to nothing. That way they will never learn how to feed on the Bible and let it inform their ideas and attitudes. You will often find people failing to apply to real life the thoughts they get from the text. So you will need to say from time to time, 'Yes, John, but I wonder what that could mean for us as we go to work tomorrow?'

I find it good to encourage people to contribute in the first person singular: 'I am excited about verse 17 because it shows me that . . .' This approach teaches people to allow the Word to penetrate beyond their intellect into their hearts, and to address them personally. As their spiritual insight grows, it is often a good idea to push them a bit further in terms of application. 'What is it you really like about that verse, Michael? What difference might it make if we actually acted on it?' It would be a good move to work over the passage in preparation, and have three or four questions up your sleeve that you could use if the contributions dry up. The best questions are those which do not allow a yes or no answer, but which stimulate discussion. Good questions can also often move the discussion to a deeper level.

Naturally there are plenty of problems you will meet in an inductive Bible study, particularly since the whole idea is so new to your group. Some people will come up with problems all the time. It may be helpful to make a teaching point out of one of these occasionally, but generally they prove a distraction from feeding on the Scriptures, which is your primary aim. You could say, 'Well, that is an interesting point, but I doubt if we have time to follow it through now. Let's get together and talk about it afterwards.' And mind you keep your word!

Then there is always sure to be a garrulous person whose plentiful contributions intimidate (or infuriate) others. 'Great, George, but you've had an opportunity to make a couple of excellent contributions already this evening . . . May we first see if someone who has not spoken yet would like to share something with us?' And how are you to help the very shy person? You must not pounce on them. Leave them quietly to absorb it all for the first couple of weeks, and thereafter venture a gentle question in their direction.

It will be a joy to see the whole group gradually getting thrilled with Scripture, and unselfconsciously discussing with one another their attempts to live it out.

Leadership in the prayer time and afterwards

The prayer time that follows is another test of your leadership. Badly introduced, it can silence one and all. But if it is led sensitively and naturally, prayer will flow. I have found it helps to say something like: 'Well, we must be drawing to a close soon. But wouldn't it be good to talk directly to the Lord before we go? We have been talking about him all evening. Let's talk to him. It is not difficult. We know how to talk to one another. We can talk to him in just the same way. Why not take a bit of Scripture that you have found spoke most clearly to you, and say a simple prayer out loud? It can be very short: "Lord, please make this true in my life" or "Thank you, God, for this." Of course, God can hear us just as well if we do not speak out loud, but others can't! And we'd like to say Amen to your prayer.' Then say, 'James [your fellow leader] will kick off, and I will close in a few minutes. But do use the time in between to pray yourself, if you would like to.' And the amazing thing is that several of them will do just that, even on the first night. I recall one person praying, 'Lord, I don't know you yet, but I want to.' It moves you to tears!

The members of the group may or may not use 'please' or 'thank you' prayers as you have suggested. They may launch out on something much more ambitious and very real. But you will have crossed a threshold that evening. Several of them will have uttered a heartfelt prayer to God, and in his mercy they will often see answers in the next few days and return the following week bubbling with enthusiasm that God does answer prayer. As the group develops you can lengthen the prayer time a little, and move on to praying for one another's needs, but never let it drag. It is amazing how speedily new Christians get into praying like this.

After the inductive Bible reading and prayer the evening is over – almost. Most of the group are in no hurry to go, and it can be quality time. You will give them their notes on the evening's events. You will find some of them browsing through the books and others wanting to start using Bible-reading notes, to help them with the beginnings of a devotional life. Some will have something they want to talk over with you.

It has been an evening of massively new experiences. Coming to a private house to talk about God, and on a weekday at that. Listening to a talk on how you can get to know God and be confident about it. Sharing where you are personally in Christian allegiance. Discovering the rudiments of Christian fellowship. Finding that the Bible speaks today. Learning a verse of Scripture by heart. Daring, maybe, to pray out loud, and really mean it. Quite an evening! Few of them will need reminders to come back next week. They will be there. But as they drift away, invite the two or three whom you are particularly looking after to a meal or a game or some such activity in the week. That will give a great opportunity for a personal chat.

Leadership in personal care

Probably during the eight-week period it takes to complete the course, you will want to have at least two sessions privately with the people entrusted to your pastoral care. The first one will be to establish relationships, and will probably begin by finding out about each other's home, interests and so forth. And then you can ask them, 'I'd love to know: have you reached the point yet in your journey when you have entrusted your life to Jesus Christ? Or are you still thinking about it?' Phrase it like that, and you will be almost certain to get an open and honest answer. Your question was not loaded. You have shown that it will be equally acceptable whichever of your options they choose. If they are not there yet, make it plain that the group meetings are likely to be a help, and that you are available to give any assistance if asked.

It is often the case that however good the public teaching in the group, your friend may simply not yet have the spiritual understanding to take it in, or the courage to make the leap of faith. And your ministrations, patiently taking her through the salient topics of the gospel until you find the sticking point, and then helping her to face and overcome it, may well lead her to that step of faith which seemed so elusive when the preacher or group leader tried to explain it in public.

It may well be the case that your friend is not ready to make any commitment as yet. In that case, encourage him to stay with the group for the full eight weeks and see what emerges. It is probable that by the end of that time he will have come to a clear faith in Christ, especially as he sees the others grow. You may like to give him something useful to read, and fix a time in two or three weeks to discuss it.

If the person is clear that he has taken that step of faith in Christ, then that first session with him should be to go through the grounds of Christian assurance again, for without that no confident Christian life can be built. You will also want to show him how to read the Bible devotionally and pray on a daily basis. Much of the modelling of this will have taken place in the group, but personal application never did anyone much harm. You may even have time to read a few verses of the Bible and pray with him there and then.

All this may require more than one session. If so, that is fine. The important thing is to give the person what they need in terms of time and advice, not to overwhelm them with it. Ideally you would hope to see them starting out with Christ, confident of it, and determined to grow with him daily.

You will need another session with your friend towards the end of the course. It can actually be quite an anxious time for members of the group. They have grown so close together that they do not view the dismantling of the group with any enthusiasm at all. You will need your skill to point them forward: to full church membership, to some area of service to undertake, and to a home group to join unless the church's policy is to stay together as a group. You will need to welcome criticisms and suggestions about the nurture group, and make it your personal responsibility to ensure that group members are properly settled in an appropriate fellowship, are growing in the Christian life, and have some sphere of ministry to pursue. Issues like work relationships, sexual mores, and use of time and money may well be worth discussing in this second personal session.

The aim is to send the person out into the full life of the church and society with a strong commitment to Christ, a firm devotional life, and a desire for both Christian fellowship and opportunities of service. This care for new Christians is an enormous privilege, and one that will test your leadership skills to the full.

The Preparation

9

The Mission –
What are the preconditions?

Let us be clear that by a mission we mean an intentional and highly specific outreach with the gospel of Christ. It may take place in a parish, a group of parishes, a university, a school or a prison, or else independently of any ecclesial structure, like the Walk of a Thousand Men. So long as you understand a mission as a clear, organised presentation of faith in Christ to those who do not know him, issuing in a challenge to do something about it, I shall not fuss about where or when it happens! In my time I have been told the Anglican *Alternative Services Book* is mission, that a sports day is mission, and so forth. No, as we saw in Chapter 1, mission in its strict sense is joining in the *missio Dei* and seeking to present the lordship of Jesus to God's unwitting, apathetic, or rebellious subjects.

But any Christian body that sets out to do this needs to go in for some self-examination first. Why do non-Christians not flock to our churches and Christian Unions? Because they do not like what they see. I am afraid it is as basic as that. The Christian church has been around for 2,000 years, and recently, in the West at any rate, it has not done a very good job of making itself the attractive, loving, generous community that Jesus intended.

Let's try, for a moment, to see ourselves as others see us. Imagine an entirely unchurched young man – let's call him Mark – who decides to investigate his local church. What do you think will strike him?

He will soon discover that the church seems to be some sort of a hierarchy, with speaking parts limited to a very few, while the rest have a walk-on part. He will be likely to find this, unfortunately, whatever denomination you think of: more in some, less in others, but in practically all of them church is centrally organised, and all the main activities are in a very few pairs of hands – normally one pair! Congregations are expected to turn up, sing up, pay up and shut up. Some individual leads the prayers and gives the sermon. That is frankly not how adults prefer to learn, at least not in our postmodern age. Mark is not very impressed.

Sermons are always part of the menu, generally a main course. But today's people do not like being talked at, and certainly not in large numbers. 'Don't you preach at me!' they say. They want to learn for themselves, and if there is a prepared talk they want their own issues to be addressed. Mark certainly does. That, after all, is why he is investigating church. But when did you last hear a sermon on a Christian attitude to the environment, or how we handle difficult ethical choices at work, or how to cope with a rebellious teenager or the loss of intimacy in a marriage? But these are some of the issues that people want help with. So words like 'irrelevant' and 'boring' are commonly applied to preaching. Mark has often heard these comments, and now he understands why. Quite a shock, really, to think that preachers have managed to make the most exciting person the world has ever seen seem dull!

The music is another turn-off in most churches. It is either semi-classical from a bygone age, with chants that nobody knows how to sing, or a collection of soppy subjective choruses whose style is equally alien to the diet of normal people like Mark.

The church building itself does not help. Many young people have never even plucked up courage to go into a church. It seems totally uncomfortable, almost spooky. And if, like Mark, they do venture in, they find their suspicions confirmed. There is even a special ecclesiastical smell! Men in suits hand the newcomer several books (I was given no fewer than four at a recent service) which he does not know what to do with. In Anglican and Roman Catholic churches the service is prescribed and written down in a large book with few explanatory notes. Other types of church do not have that problem, but there is generally a predictability about the proceedings, even how many minutes the sermon is tolerated. Mark begins to realise that a formal liturgy is only one of the many captivities of the church.

Mark would probably find that apart from a greeting at the door nobody would speak to him, even over the watery coffee in green cups that follows the service. He would, after a few visits, begin to suspect that the choir was singing not so much to the glory of God but of themselves. He might well begin to stumble upon the tensions in the church, classically between the minister and the organist, but if not there, somewhere else. There is talk of prayer but it does not seem to be a priority in the actual worship meetings, and who knows if anyone does it at home? Similarly the Bible is much venerated, but Mark has a shrewd suspicion that some of the people who get up each Sunday and read it have not a clue what it is all about. Neither does the joy which Christians are supposed to have seem very plentiful as Mark glances at the faces of people leaving church.

Another thing that puzzles him is that most of those who go to church are either very old or very young. The over-sixties and the under-sixes predominate. But perhaps there aren't even any kids under six in church. Many churches have no youth work of any kind. It is all very odd. Mark asks himself why the main active age group of society does not go to church, and why there are twice as many women as men.

As he moves around among the coffee drinkers after the service, he notices that there is very little talk about God and the difference he is supposed to make to life. It is never discussed. Folk seem to get onto more normal topics of the weather and the news as soon as they can. In most churches there is no induction course for someone like him who is trying to examine the Christian faith. Apparently you are expected to come to a church service and either sink or swim.

After a while, Mark comes to the conclusion that there is very little difference in lifestyle between churchpeople and those who claim no Christian allegiance. The Christians are no more generous, loving, unselfish or sacrificial of time and money than the cheery pagans who never go near the church. That seems to him a very strange thing when such great claims are made for the transformation Christ is supposed to bring.

The above may be a slight caricature, but it is not massive exaggeration. There are a great many churches rather like that. Just imagine what a disaster it would be if one of them realised that there are lots of empty seats where once there were people, and decided to have a mission. What would happen?

The insiders would resent the disturbance, and keep their heads well down beneath the parapet until this mission thing had gone away. They would then emerge, and complain vociferously. The outsiders would make one visit to such a church and decide 'No thanks: not my scene.'

You cannot embark on a mission and just hope that some good will come of it. Only recently I had an invitation of that sort. The vicar recalled a mission that was held a decade ago and apparently deepened the spiritual life of the congregation. Glad to hear it. But that is not the main object of a mission. It is to reach beyond the church to friends and neighbours who do not know Christ. This vicar apparently had no plans for that. Needless to say, I politely declined. Outreach has no hope of being effective if the interior life of the church is low. Often I have been asked to lead a mission in such a church and have had to refuse, knowing that it would be useless because of the spiritual state of the church. I am perfectly willing, however, diary permitting, to give some extended teaching on elements that are essential in any church that hopes to impact its community through a carefully prepared mission. Only after those are in place, to some discernible degree, will a mission be any good.

What I look for is a church that has begun to address the following:

1. *The ability to cope with change.* Is this church so set in its ways that it regards all change as a threat, or is there a willingness to trust God and take risks?

2. *Lively, sincere and varied worship.* Is there a sense that God is around and in business when the congregation

meets for worship – whatever style that worship may be? Today's searchers are very sensitive to spiritual reality, and are apt to spot 'the Beyond in the midst' rather faster than some churchpeople.

3. *Evidence of love and friendship in the church.* Is it a place of welcome and laughter, of warm relationships, mutual understanding and forgiveness? Love is the language of heaven. And unless there is some of it flowing through a church, it is not going to attract anyone to God.

4. *A concern for the locality and its needs.* Is the church introverted and concerned only with its small affairs? Or has it a heart that reaches out with practical service to try to meet the genuine needs of people in its vicinity – and beyond? It may have very limited resources, but is there practical evidence of that longing to look beyond itself and help?

5. *Generosity in giving and serving.* A lively church is a generous church. God is allowed to touch the pockets of his grateful people. And in the same way, if they have been moved by what God has done for them, they will be wanting to serve him according to the talents and abilities each one has. The aim in any flourishing congregation is 'every member ministry', for every Christian is called to serve the Lord in some way or other.

6. *Structures to enable members to share their lives.* I am thinking primarily, but not exclusively, of small groups in the life of the church. But there need to be some structures which make it easy for members to speak about what God is doing in their lives, to share their news, pray

together and encourage each other. Once they are comfortable doing this with one another, the confidence of the church grows and it is a comparatively small step to go on to approach those who are not yet Christians.

7. *Evidence of prayer life.* It does not matter whether it is silent or spoken prayer, prayer walks or prayer triplets, concerts of prayer, nights of payer or prayer retreats. But prayer is vital. And prayer must be directed beyond the life of the church. Without that, no mission will have a chance. I encourage church members to write a list of four or five names of people whom they long to invite to something during the mission. It is amazing how strange this seems to many who have been churchpeople all their lives.

8. *Care for the needy in the congregation.* These may be the aged and infirm, the overburdened mother with four kids, the handicapped, the impoverished. But does the congregation care enough to help them? That is a very significant indicator of spiritual life.

9. *Is there a 'nursery'?* By that I do not mean a nursery for small kids during the service, though that is an invaluable feature, but a congenial means for those enquiring about Christianity, or those who are new believers, to meet, question, grow and be helped along the road.

10. *Are new members joining?* I learnt a marvellous new phrase when working in Canada: 'sheep-shuffling'. This refers to the very light attachment many Christians have to their church, and their readiness to go down the road to another one that is the flavour of the month. Anyone can grow a church that way! But are any new people

becoming Christians through the work of the church? That is what I want to know. It does not need to be many, but if the church never sees any conversions, then a mission is likely to be too strong a medicine.

11. *Is there any youth and children's work?* Astonishingly, a high proportion of churches in Britain have little or no children's work, no Sunday school, no youth fellowship. They are devoid of young people. This is a tragedy, and generally means there are no adults in the church who care enough to give love and time to winning the confidence of youngsters and drawing them towards the faith. And when you remember that the majority of people come to faith while they are children or teenagers, this is a disaster. So the presence of some youth work, however rudimentary, and the willingness of some volunteers to run it, is rather important if you want to have a mission.

12. *Does the church actually believe the biblical faith?* That may seem an unnecessary question, but unfortunately it is not. Many churches have been weaned off biblical Christianity by the spirit of the age. But unless there is some confidence in the Bible as the source book of our faith, unless there is some willingness for biblical emphases such as the new birth and the challenge of commitment to be preached in the mission and underlined in the church, then it is much better not to start. St Paul writes in distress to the Galatians who were 'turning to a different gospel – not that there is another gospel'. He continues, 'If anyone preaches to you a gospel contrary to what you have received, let him be accursed.' Strong words, to be sure, and strong convictions. But all over the world you will find that the only Christianity

which is consistently growing is the Christianity based on the Bible. And any missioner worth his salt needs to have freedom and enthusiastic backing to preach unvarnished New Testament Christianity. Not all churches can stomach that.

Please do not think that this is a narrow-minded checklist and that churches are judged by their answers to these questions. These are only some of the straws in the wind that are helpful in deciding whether it will be profitable to have a mission. They are indicators of life, and only a church that shares something of the life of Jesus can attract others to him who is the Way, the Truth and the Life.

10

The Mission –
How can we prepare?

Imparting the vision

Sometimes I have been disappointed at the results of a mission into which a lot of prayer and hard work has gone. The invitation to me had been warm, the minister enthusiastic, the plans imaginative. But little came of it. Churchpeople did not bring their friends. We were quite literally preaching to the converted. What was wrong?

The trouble comes when the vision has never been shared and owned by the congregation. If a mission is to be effective, virtually the entire congregation needs to be determined to move ahead together. Consequently the minister must do a good deal of teaching about it beforehand, whetting the appetites of the congregation to see their friends come to Christian faith. And they must not just be convinced that this is a good thing; they must be willing to be involved themselves in praying, inviting, hospitality and commitment to the enterprise. Naturally you cannot expect the whole congregation to get the vision – they never do. But unless the minister, the PCC (or other leadership team), and the majority of the congregation get on board, the mission is doomed to failure.

Taking a mission audit

A few years ago 'drawing up our mission audit' became a fashionable cliché. But actually there was nothing special about it. It simply means taking careful stock of the numbers and type of people, their main age groups, job situations and common leisure interests, together with schools and other institutions and organisations in the geographical area where the mission is to be held, and then matching those discoveries with the strengths and weaknesses of the local church.

I heard of a minister not long ago bemoaning the fact that he had no youth work, and feeling, as a result, that he was a terrible failure. But a demographic study of the area showed that very few young people lived there: it was predominantly an older population. No wonder he had no youth work! It is no good laying on an event, however scintillating, if there are no appropriate customers around.

I have been very struck in my work in south east Asia to see how carefully the Christians, who have a passion for evangelism, do a detailed study of their community before they attempt anything. In the West, I fear, we are more casual. As a result the membership of the congregation, which is after all voluntary and to some extent haphazard, may well not represent at all accurately a cross-section of the local community. Careful demographics, though perhaps boring, are essential if the mission is to hit the target. This will enable the leadership to decide whether to have a mission to the parish as a whole, or to aim for a homogeneous unit. It might be directed to the youth, to sportsmen and women, to business people, to the retired. Find out what type of people you are aiming to reach, and make that discovery fundamental to all your plans.

Once you are clear about your aim, you can then move on to consider questions like the length of the mission: should it last a week, two weeks, or perhaps three separate weekends? Should it concentrate on large meetings, which are less and less effective these days, or seek to approach different interest and age groups in the milieu in which they are most at home? This is usually a more promising approach. A variation would be to concentrate almost the whole outreach on small home groups, spawned by members of the church inviting their friends to come round. Most missions with which I have been involved in all five continents have gone for a mixture of the above, with home groups, interest groups, fun events, pub meetings, and a few large gatherings, together with the Sunday services. The time of year may well be critical, too, as may the major commitments of key members of your church.

Choosing a mission leader

At this stage you may be ready to choose your mission leader, carefully matching his or her known gifts against the needs you have discerned in your mission audit. A great deal hangs on whom you invite. There must be real trust between such a person and the local leadership. A mission can fail if people in the congregation do not know the person chosen and do not have confidence in him or her. After all, folk are not going to risk their friends on someone in whom they have no confidence. So the choice is critical. The minister and lay leaders will, if they are wise, draw up a list of names, and if possible some of the leadership team should go and hear them speak. They are trying to find the human channel most appropriate for their own situation. You may not succeed in getting your first choice, so it is sensible to identify three or four people who could be appropriate. The Church of England has given (belated!) help in this matter, carefully selecting for its College of Evangelists those who have a proven track record for evangelism beyond their home church. That could be a useful pool to fish in.

Making a first impression

You only get one chance to make a first impression, and so the initial visit of the chosen mission leader to the congregation or university is very important. It is helpful to combine his or her first appearance with a main Sunday service or meeting if at all possible, so that the congregation can begin to get to know and trust him. He, on his part, will be keen to explain the need for a mission, how it fits in with the ongoing life of the church, and roughly what strategy is envisaged. He will also need to begin to teach them about the value of bringing a team with him during the mission. They may well still harbour the idea that a mission involves the congregation dragging their friends to church to be preached at by a single individual. They need to be disabused of this idea!

After his visit, the leadership of the church should send him a confirmation of their invitation and an undertaking to support the mission at all levels.

Thereafter the mission needs to be given an increasingly high profile in the notices of the church or Christian fellowship so that all members begin to grasp the vision and begin to see where they fit in. It is no bad idea for someone other than the minister to do this, partly so that the mission does not look like his or her personal hobby, and partly because someone else can concentrate exclusively on the mission in a way the minister cannot because of other duties.

Planning the build-up

Now is the time to begin detailed planning. It should start at least nine months beforehand, and preferably more, so that everyone can fully understand the goals (and the dates) of the mission, and begin to reflect on their part in it.

It is at this juncture that misunderstandings are likely to crop up. The minister may feel it is all his responsibility, or alternatively may want to delegate all responsibility to others. There may be vestigial remains of outdated perceptions of mission. There may be different expectations among the visiting team and the local church. Much care needs to be given to working together in harmony.

Money often rears its ugly head. It is vital that the leadership is clear on the financial issue. Is the parish expected to pay for the visiting team or not? Does the missioner expect a fee? I would not be against the latter: St Paul sometimes accepted support from those he ministered to, and at other times he declined. And some independent evangelists have no guaranteed income apart from what they receive through events like this. Personally I prefer to charge nothing for the mission. It then comes as a free gift, like the gospel it proclaims. But there is a proper partnership in giving. The team comes for nothing, but expects to be fed and accommodated by the local congregation. The visitors give their efforts freely and gladly, and the recipients give their hospitality free of charge. It is a good policy wherever possible, and it leaves a nice taste in the mouth. Nobody can accuse the missioner of being on the make. I think it is fitting that the receiving institution should pay travelling expenses at an agreed rate, and of course pay for publicity at their end. Whatever the decision, it should be clearly understood and adhered to by both parties.

I also find it helpful if all money-raising is done before the mission happens. People suspect the church of making money out of them, and joke about the collection that is made at every event. Let's surprise them by having no collections. I do not want people to pay to be evangelised! Raise the money beforehand, and make the needs known in the congregation. There will be several folk who will come up with personal cheques for evangelism: they care about it. Often the church feels it cannot raise the money. Well, they will be surprised when they do, and that will build faith and confidence. I have led scores of missions and I have never known one that did not balance the books. If the mission is really in God's plan the money will be forthcoming. He is no man's debtor, and he pays for what he orders.

If money is one possible cause for misunderstanding, programme is another. Churchpeople often expect the missioner to have a package, his way of doing things, which he imposes willy-nilly on the recipients. That way lies disaster. In my initial meetings with the parish, I sometimes hold up a blank piece of paper and say, 'These are my plans for the mission!' When they have got over the shock, we then sit down and begin to plan together. In this way they do not feel that something is being foisted upon them.

In planning, it is usually best to do two things. First, to

try to reach outwards from all areas in which the church is strong and has good links with unchurched people. And second, bearing in mind the demographics of the area, to consider what institutions or groups of people, where Christian influence is currently weak or non-existent, should be given special attention during the mission. If bridgeheads can be established here, they can be developed in the months that follow the mission.

Having cleared out of the way possible causes of misunderstanding such as these, a title for the mission needs to be concocted. It should be short and pithy, attractive and related to the locality rather than the visiting missioner. It must be designed to arrest and appeal to people outside the church.

It is also a good idea to produce a short written document for the congregation at this point, and to produce a sequel every month or so, in order that there be no misunderstanding in the congregation about what is going on, and that they may be kept in the picture about the development of the plans. This may be a bit of a nuisance, but it pays handsomely.

The local minister could helpfully sit down at this point with trusted colleagues and plan the teaching and preaching programme for the months until the mission, concentrating on the Lord's Great Commission, the need of those without Christ, the joy of bearing witness, and God's reliance on the faithfulness of his church. There could also be helpful teaching on the need for every-member ministry and some insight into the different gifts which members could bring to bear. This teaching leading up to the mission underlines the fact that the church regards outreach as very important and is determined to prioritise it.

The most important requirement in the build-up to a

mission is prayer. In prayer we confess to God that we cannot bring anyone to faith: that is the work of God alone. We are totally dependent on him, and show it by our prayers. There needs to be teaching on intercessory prayer. Most Christians pray for God's blessing on their nearest and dearest, and perhaps for the church they attend, but not much further afield. Few are strong in meditation and thanksgiving, let alone confession. But one of our greatest weaknesses in prayer is failure to pray regularly for our friends and neighbours who do not know Christ. This weakness must be tackled. There needs to be teaching on prayer, and prayer groups and parish prayer times need to be mobilised for the mission – and you will find they will continue afterwards, and fertilise the work of the church.

The Archbishops' Initiative in Evangelism, Springboard, has come up with some attractive little cards, called Oikos cards (from the Greek for household and friends), with half a dozen blanks on for people to write in the names of those they long to see converted in the mission, and a reminder to pray regularly for them. They may be ordered in bulk from Springboard, 4 Old Station Yard, Abingdon OX14 3LD. Springboard also publishes a splendid booklet on one type of parish mission, *Preparing for Mission Weekends*, which may be obtained from the same source and is full of wise advice.

Prayer is the right note on which to end this chapter. I recall a mission in Canada some years ago, and one of our team, a Ghanaian girl, preached her heart out in a Lutheran church. The minister was visibly moved, and he asked her to get back into the pulpit and explain to people how they prepared for a mission in Ghana. She was very reluctant to do so. But eventually she agreed. She told them that most of the preparation we do in the

West they leave undone. But they pray. They often spend whole nights in prayer before a mission. 'That is how we prepare,' she said, 'and we find that God has prepared the way for us and many come to faith.' Heads drooped. The congregation knew how far we in the West fall short of that standard.

There are at least three other essential elements in preparing for a mission, and we shall look at them in the next chapter.

11

The Task Force –
How shall we set it up?

The Mission Task Force

A great deal of work needs to go on within the receiving parish or university in terms of preparation. The better and more thorough the preparation, the more effective the mission. Most missions suffer from lack of detailed preparation.

First and foremost, I believe, is the appointment of a Task Force. I do not call it an organising committee, because the mentality of committees is to discuss and report back. The mentality needed here is to plan and act. It is sheer folly to rely on the minister to handle it all, because there is much to be done – far more than one person can achieve. It is best to form a largely lay Task Force to get ready for the mission. This may well mean their being relieved temporarily of their regular jobs in the church, in order to allow them to concentrate on the mission without unduly encroaching on family time or daily workload.

This must be a working Task Force. We should choose people because they have the requisite gifts for the different jobs, not because of their standing in the church. Certain areas must be covered: prayer, finance, publicity, youth work, events, hospitality, counselling and follow up. Other areas may well emerge as the plans take shape. Some of these tasks can be handled by a single individual, but there is much to be said for forming little sub-groups which can handle different aspects of the appropriate portfolio: for example, on the hospitality front one person could handle the accommodation of the team, and another their meals. Each of the sub-groups works in its own area and is represented on the Task Force by its co-ordinator.

The chairperson needs to be selected with especial care: someone who enjoys wide respect, and has a level head and good interpersonal skills. The chair needs to be able to motivate the congregation and shape the course which the mission may take. He or she needs to be able tactfully to oversee the portfolios of the rest of the Task Force, ensuring that progress is made by the agreed time. It is often helpful to have a flow chart of what needs to be done with target dates.

A *vice-chair* is also very important, to work alongside the chair and share in the responsibility. He or she may also undertake a particular portfolio. If the chair is ordained, the vice-chair should be a layperson. There is, of course, no reason why the chair should be a minister, unless chairmanship happens to be his or her obvious gift: some clergy are hopeless in such a role. Either the chair or the vice-chair needs to be charged with the job of keeping in regular touch with the missioner. Emails make this very easy, and facilitate the immediate dissemination of information to the Task Force as a whole.

A *secretary* for the Task Force is vital. Ideally this could be the church secretary unless they are already overloaded. She or he will know every detail of church life and will be able to give invaluable background information to the missioner as well as keep and circulate minutes of the Task Force meetings.

The prayer co-ordinator needs to be someone passionately convinced of the power of prayer and able to motivate others to pray. The co-ordinator might introduce prayer triplets, encouraging groups of three Christians to meet weekly to pray for friends of theirs who are not yet Christians. Then a prayer card should be prepared for widespread use in the congregation, with major mission topics on one side and space for people to put names of friends on the other. Part of the prayer co-ordinator's task is to ensure that prayer by the congregation for the mission takes place in church each week, and to supply news as it emerges. Finally, of course, the prayer co-ordinator needs to organise prayer meetings, concerts of prayer, or half nights of prayer for the mission. All too often in Christian work, the words of St James come true: 'You do not have because you do not ask'.

Publicity is another vital element, and is best dealt with by a small team with different publicity skills. You want to get into the local paper, the local radio and if possible local TV, and bend all energies both to publicise the mission among the congregation and to reach the wider community. Artwork must be produced as required, along with the design and production of all posters required for the mission. Quantities of handbills will need to be available as the mission draws near, with details of the main events on them. Some will be distributed house-to-house, but more will need to be placed in the hands of the visiting team for those they meet. In addition, the publicity team must produce an adequate PA system for the mission itself. Of course, the best means of publicity is by word of mouth, and the publicity co-ordinator should take great pains to encourage enthusiasm among the congregation so that lots of informal conversation and invitations may ensue.

Youth work is critical. There is a massive bleeding of young people away from almost all the traditional churches in the country. Many of the New Churches are doing rather better: they recognise the need of appointing a youth pastor, which is normal in America but rare in Britain. Those who are leading the youth and children's work in the church need to be involved with the Task Force from the outset, and to start planning a programme for the teenagers and children.

They could organise a concert with a guest artist who has skills not only in music but in presenting the challenge of Christ. They could have a sports evening in the mission incorporating one of the Christians in Sport videos, in which leading sportsmen and women speak of their faith in Christ. They could plan and host a barbecue, a sports day, a concert, or whatever else might fit in with the interests of the young people with whom they are in touch. They may well be able to give out initial publicity in the local schools. The visiting team, of course, is likely to comprise several members who are expert in youth work, and this needs to be explored and taken into account early in the planning. Often it is possible for the visiting team to take school assemblies, and be grilled about their Christian faith in classes at the school. The youth co-ordinator should carefully explore every avenue – after-school concerts or meetings, lunchtime events, sixth form question times and so forth.

The hospitality sub-group will be concerned with two things. First, where team members will be accommodated, and whether it is for bed and breakfast only, or also for the evening meal. The other side of the job is to arrange for a simple lunch to be provided daily. This is best done in a central location, so it offers not only food but an opportunity for fellowship and temporary relaxation among the team itself.

Counselling and follow-up is an important part of mission planning. It is a vital and delicate job. Delicate because with memories of Billy Graham's crusades in their minds, some of the more enthusiastic members of the congregation are likely to want to 'counsel' enquirers after the mission events, expecting people to be invited forward by the evangelist. But this happens much less these days: there are other more sensitive ways of eliciting response. So if a church trains a whole raft of counsellors to be armed with a number of questions, an evangelistic booklet and a gospel, they are likely to be disappointed. Most of the immediate dealing with concerned people after meetings will be done by team members themselves, and their names passed to the church for careful follow-up after the mission is over.

My experience is that the best way of gathering the fruits of a mission is through the use of response cards, which we use at every meeting, and when we have good chance contacts with individuals. These cards simply give space for name, address and phone number, rough age group, church link if any, and a number of boxes which can be ticked. These can vary according to the requirements of the university or parish, but generally one of them is for seekers: 'I am interested in finding out more about Christianity'. One is for those who want a visit: 'I would be grateful for someone from the church (or CU) to visit me'. And one is for those who want to indicate commitment to Christ: 'I have today entrusted my life to Jesus Christ'. Of course, you can have more boxes: 'I am not convinced. Please invite me to a discussion group' or

'Please invite me to a short course on Christian discipleship' – but the more boxes you have, the more confusing the card becomes.

I shall have more to say about the card later on, because it needs to be used with skill. But it is an invaluable tool because it leaves behind in the parish a record of the best work done by the mission team. Without it, any impact they may have had disappears into thin air. So the follow-up co-ordinator will need to plan the precise wording of the card with the missioner, and then see that adequate numbers are printed, and that more can be run off if required. He will also plan with the local minister to see that nurture groups are in place immediately the mission is over. That will involve training people to lead such groups. And it is a real act of faith, because there will probably be nobody in these groups as yet. When the names begin to appear during the mission, much tact and insight will be needed to place them in the appropriate nurture groups.

Missions cost money, so *a finance portfolio* is essential. If the visiting team is not interested in any remuneration, the costs are likely to be very reasonable. There will be transport costs for the team, both in getting to the locality and while working there. There will be publicity costs and perhaps the hiring of rooms or PA equipment. And there will be some food costs, though most hosts will not ask for payment for putting up a team member, and the mid-day lunches can be produced very cheaply by volunteers in the congregation. So the finance should not be a great problem. Also you often find in a congregation a few people who really care about evangelism and offer a substantial personal donation. I encourage parishes to have all the finance in place before the mission begins, if at all possible. I hate any collection at an evangelistic service. Perhaps the exception is the last night, when many people have been blessed by the mission and may want to make a thank-offering.

The events co-ordinator is perhaps the final essential member of the Task Force. He or she will keep track of events. These will include every event at which a team member is expected to appear. This is a job that requires an organised mind! It would be wise to devise proformas for home meetings, schools meetings, services, and other events which will be handed out to those involved, so that the events co-ordinator gradually amasses a large number of these forms, recording events large and small at which a team member is required. These need to be communicated to the missioner a couple of weeks before the mission at the latest, so that he can assign the most suitable team speakers to these occasions, and they can prepare properly beforehand. Often people will ask for a particular speaker from the team at their event. The events co-ordinator should gently defer a decision. This avoids the 'early birds' exercising undue pressure, and leaves the final decision for any event in the hands of the missioner, who will know his team well. It is impossible to exaggerate the importance of this portfolio. If enough small meetings are not mounted by the congregation, the mission will be useless. It is imperative to have relaxed contact with non-church people, and the only ones who can bring that about are their Christian friends. Small, informal home meetings are so easy to arrange, and yet people are so loath to arrange them. The tact, humour and charm of the events co-ordinator will be fully stretched if enough events are to be arranged where there is real contact with non-churchgoers. The missioners do not want simply to meet groups of other Christians.

The inter-church Task Force

Increasingly these days I find that a whole variety of churches are willing to band together in an outreach such as we have been suggesting. The denominational barriers are much lower than they used to be. Christians of all stripes realise that in a world which is indifferent or opposed to Christianity we need to pull together. Disunity and competition are luxuries we cannot allow ourselves – and never should have done. And so I find Roman Catholics and Methodists, URC members and Anglicans, New Church members and Baptists are often willing to combine to bring the gospel of Christ to the area. This need not involve any compromise in belief – simply the recognition that the things which unite us are far greater than the things which divide. I rejoice to see denominational barriers dropping, and different churches laying aside their particular emphasis for a week and joining together for the cause of the King and the kingdom.

When, therefore, I am asked to lead a single church mission I always seek to broaden it across the denominations. It then gives us the right to approach the mayor and tell him that as the churches are all combining to spread the gospel in the town, we would be glad to have an opportunity of addressing him and his aldermen. I find that mayors are usually so surprised at this Christian unity in mission that they readily agree, and may offer a reception in the Parlour!

In order to set up a town-wide mission, it must first be agreed at a meeting of the local ministers. The vision will need to be imparted and it will need to be made plain that no single package is envisaged, but that co-operating churches will be served by the mission team in a way that suits their own situation. Again the point will need to be stressed that this sort of mission is not based on a single individual but on a team, working alongside local Christians to permeate every level of society.

The missioner will then need to explain what is required of participating churches. They will need to indicate their involvement by an agreed date, with the backing of their church's decision-making body. They will agree to finance the venture, as before, and will undertake to allow team members full access to every type of regular church event.

In addition they will put on three additional types of event. First, there will be one or two combined events for all of the church communities as they reach out into their area. This may mean a venue which holds hundreds or perhaps even thousands. Second, each church will put on one or more special major events at which the visiting team will provide (or import for the occasion) an accomplished speaker. And third, there must be scores of small groups in homes, work places, schools and so forth. Furthermore, there must be agreement from the outset as to what will follow the mission. Two possibilities are obvious. One would mean that each church runs its own nurture groups. The other goes further in the realm of trust and partnership, and agrees to nurture groups that are run transdenominationally. But this must be made clear from the outset, or else there are sure to be cries of sheep-stealing, and that would be dishonouring to God and not at all the purpose of a mission.

Given these conditions, the organisation of a town-wide mission runs on very similar lines to those we have been discussing for a single church. It is important to have an occasional meeting of ministers to review progress, but the actual planning and detailed preparation should be in the hands of a Task Force whose members are not chosen so much to achieve a denominational balance but rather for the skills they have to offer for the different portfolios. The Task Force will probably need to meet monthly to begin with, and then more frequently as the mission approaches.

The chairperson's role is even more arduous, ensuring inter-church relationships of high quality. It is also their job to be in regular touch with the lay representatives from each church. I find that such people are essential if the vision is to be grasped by each church as a whole. The lay representative, who may well also be the church's prayer co-ordinator, needs access to the chair for accurate information, advice and encouragement. The chairperson also needs to find occasions for the members of the Task Force to have a relaxed and enjoyable time together, since good decisions emerge from good relationships.

The vice-chair's role remains the same, and it is important for him and the chairperson to work closely together in overseeing the whole enterprise, and to keep in close contact with the missioner. I find it almost invariable that slightly different ideas for running a mission emerge at a local level from those that are in the mind of the missioner, and this can lead to unnecessary misunderstanding and even recrimination when the mission takes place. Close liaison is vital.

The programme co-ordinator needs both pastoral and organisational gifts. He or she will be responsible for keeping in touch with all those in the different churches who are planning programme activities; for imaginatively facilitating major events for the mission; and for drawing the whole programme together for presentation to the missioner. Because of the importance of small meetings in a large inter-church event, it may well be a good idea to have someone else working as a small meetings co-ordinator, responsible for mobilising, encouraging, and keeping a record of literally hundreds of small meetings in the co-operating churches. A proforma should be produced as suggested above, and every host should fill it out. This enables accurate and adequate information reaching the missioner. Without it, chaos will ensue!

The finance co-ordinator will need to draw up a budget, to be shared among the participating churches, preferably depending on their size. Because there are a lot of initial expenses to get a large venture like this off the ground, it will be his role to seek an initial contribution from all the participating churches, and let them know when the residue should be paid. Again it is worth emphasising that God pays for what he orders. I have never known a venture like this (including three major city-wide examples) to be short of cash at the end.

The youth co-ordinator will have a rare opportunity of getting all the youth leaders in the area together, and working out an agreed strategy. This may well involve their importing youth experts unless there are really gifted youth workers on the team the missioner will be bringing. If close fellowship, first among the youth leaders and then among their charges, is fostered, it could lead to a large monthly youth rally in the area after the mission. This is something which can really catch on among young people. It has reached monumental proportions, for example, in Manchester under Andy Hawthorne and The Message Tribe. The quality of something like this will far exceed the resources of any single youth group, but it cannot happen unless there is real trust and co-operation among youth workers. A mission is an ideal opportunity to work on this.

The role of the *hospitality co-ordinator* will be much the same as in the single church mission. He or she will be responsible for the housing of the team and its meals. The missioner will supply a list of team members, with details of their gender, denomination, age and any food allergies. It is good to recruit hosts from among the fringe of the churches if possible, so that a team member can be a godly advertisement in a home where perhaps only one member is a Christian. Clarify to the hosts what is expected of them, and send the addresses of hosts to the missioner before the team arrives. The co-ordinator may well find it easiest to ask different participating churches to provide the mid-day meal on specific days, so as to share the load.

The work of the *prayer co-ordinator* will be expanded in an inter-church venture. He or she will need to visit each participating church to mobilise meetings for prayer and ensure that a local prayer co-ordinator is active in each church. It will also be good to take an opportunity to speak on the power of prayer and to defuse misunderstandings about the mission. Interdenominational prayer meetings are important, so as to encourage a deep sense of partnership among churches that have probably hitherto lived in isolation from one another. Chains of prayer across town, and a town-wide concert of prayer (short bursts of directed praise and prayer) before the mission will be important building blocks. A simple news-sheet devised to go into church bulletins with prayer and praise items is another help. If joint corporate prayer catches fire, the churches in town will never be the same again.

All of this simply underlines the force of Jesus' teaching in John 17, that prayer, unity and mission go together. Unbelievers will never be won without prayer, for God alone can convert. And they will never be won without seeing the unity and love of the Christian churches in the area.

12

The Team – How can we train them? Part 1

We have looked at what needs to be done by way of preparation in the parish. What about the missioner and his team?

Choosing the team

The first task of the evangelist is to choose a team. Sometimes it is easy. Some evangelists work with a regular team, and this becomes the core to which others may be added. Currently, I work within a theological college, and it is natural to take ordinands with me on a mission. It is an invaluable part of their training. But I was impressed when I worked for Springboard, the initiative started in 1992 by the Archbishops for evangelism in Britain, that all sorts of people wrote in to us asking if they could come on a mission. There are many people who are keen to share their faith in the intentional way that a mission affords.

I am struck by the rugged, raw talent of the men whom Daniel Cozens gathers each year for the Walk of a Thousand Men. Men who have been on these missions, walk-

ing along a pre-planned route and using pubs as the main
places for explaining the good news, gain enormously
from the experience. Indeed, they have now become so
numerous that they are acting as unpaid ministers in
many a small church up and down the land where no
clergyman is available. And their training has come
entirely from missions with Daniel. It shows what can be
done with vision and dedication. There are many ways of
gathering a team, and such is the general dearth of evangelistic initiatives that when someone steps forward as a
leader he rarely lacks volunteers from within the Christian community.

But the selection of a team must be done with care.
You need some who are evangelists, some who are
musicians and dramatists, some who make people laugh
and others who are skilled with young people or elderly
people. Some should be good at speaking in small home
groups, and others in the open air. A balanced team of
young and older men and women from a variety of back-
grounds is a great blessing. It is worth working for.

Bonding the team

The next priority is to bond the team together. This gradually emerges through regular, relaxed meetings in which all
available information is shared, so that everyone has equal
insight into the project and shares a sense of ownership.

It is important early on to have a full discussion of the
gifts and background of all the team members, so that we
all know each other's strengths and life experience. This
makes an enormous difference when selecting people for
assignments during the mission. It also helps within the
team itself for members to know each other's story as it
makes for mutual interdependence.

Bonding is deepened by prayer. It is essential that a good deal of time is given in each team meeting to prayer, and that members pledge to pray regularly for the mission.

Preparing the team

The team may well not have worked together before, so it is important to understand and maximise the talents of each member. Every team leader will handle it in his own way, but I like to choose one or perhaps two highly respected members who will help me lead the team. They will mobilise prayer meetings, handle a good deal of the correspondence and join with me during the mission itself in allotting members to assignments.

I like to discover who the musicians are, and ask one of them to organise a music group. This is primarily for worship at the daily meetings of the team during the mission, but may also have a further purpose of giving some public musical presentations during the mission.

I believe very much in the power of drama and mime to drive home the message of the gospel. This is particularly important in a postmodern age when there is a good deal of cynicism about the spoken word, but interest in drama, dance, song and mime as means of communication. Often there will be team members with considerable experience of drama; one of them needs to be put in charge of a group within the team who are willing to prepare half a dozen or so short dramatic sketches which point up some aspect of the gospel, and can be used to illuminate and give fresh dynamism to talks during the mission. The pioneers in this area were Riding Lights, and a number of their sketches are available, but many others have been writing these short, challenging pieces which make one point vividly and leave the speaker to develop the theme. I have a good many of these sketches, and find that when I ask a drama team to get to work they may also come up with suitable material. Because of the pressures upon the whole team during the mission, it is desirable, if at all possible, that the majority of the sketches are learnt beforehand.

You may also have some team member who is good at circle dancing. If so, it is not difficult to teach the team, and the impact of a large and lively circle dance in a town street is enormous. It celebrates the exuberant joy of the Christian life, and the partnership of those engaged in it. It makes many curious. They stop, wonder, and perhaps revise their opinion of Christianity.

It is important also to appoint someone in charge of transport, to sort out who goes with whom travelling to the mission, and present consolidated accounts of petrol costs to the mission treasurer at the end.

Training the team

There are at least five areas in which members of a mission team need to have some competence. They must be able to handle a home meeting, to explain convincingly what Christ means to them, to give an attractive and challenging evangelistic talk, to work with some insight in the open air, and to give a public address. In this chapter and the next we shall look at these in turn.

Leading a house meeting

Many home meetings will emerge during a mission, where local Christians have invited their friends. Remember that almost everyone who is present will be a minor triumph: the British are reluctant to come to a meeting where God may become the focus! It is important that they enjoy and profit from the experience. These meetings are the bread and butter of a mission. They enable team members to meet with people in a context where it is easier to talk one to one about the faith.

The hosts will have been encouraged to invite their not-yet-Christian friends to meet informally with a couple of team members. These meetings can take place over any meal, coffee, or even in a jacuzzi. After people have been given refreshments, the host will introduce the team members (it is usual for them to be sent out two by two) and then hand over to the team.

The team members will already have contacted the hosts the day before, allayed their fears, and given them confidence. They will find out as much as they can about those who are expected. They will agree with the hosts about the aim of the meeting – some meetings will be much more pre-evangelistic than others. They will survey the room where the meeting will be held, and perhaps suggest a drink after the meeting to enable people to stay there for a little, while personal conversations take place: these are usually the most important part of the whole event. Hosts are rarely quite sure who will be coming. Encourage them to phone people before the meeting to remind them, and to keep praying.

The team members should decide which of them is actually going to lead the meeting, and what form it should take. It may be best for each of them to say something about themselves, including their encounter with Christ, and then invite others present to share something of their stories. It may work for one of the pair to give a short arresting talk, and then for his colleague to earth it by saying what Christ has done for him personally, before leading into discussion. Alternatively, it may be good to open the whole thing to questions people have always wondered about. Whatever the plan, make sure that both of you are clear about it.

It is vital in these home meetings to get people involved. It is not the occasion to practise your best sermon! Until you know what the guests are really feeling it is not possible to speak directly into their situation. So their active participation is vital.

Another wise move is to take the outlines of two talks with you. You will plan to give one if there are indeed non-Christians present. But you will give the other if they have all ducked out, and all that are left are a few discouraged Christians who tried hard to invite their friends, but in vain. They do not need to be chided, but encouraged, and shown other ways of reaching their friends. I often find that these occasions when non-Christians do not show up are marvellous for really encouraging the Christians present and giving them new vision and confidence.

Remember that people come to a meeting like this for a variety of reasons. Some are curious, some militant, while others are there only because they don't want to offend the hosts. Many of them will be apprehensive. It is a top priority to put them at their ease. Some will have a living testimony, others no faith at all. Do not get into an argument, or allow others to do so. There is a great difference between unprofitable argument and lively discussion. Relationships with the people are much more important than winning the point at issue.

In the discussion, try not to dominate, but be prepared to change the direction if needed. Draw your colleague in. Do not be embarrassed to answer questions from Scripture: it is powerful. Avoid the situation where questions are all addressed to team members. Open it up for others to contribute – and do not allow one person to dominate. Keep in touch with the Holy Spirit, and expect the unexpected. And at some point, the way of salvation in Christ needs to be clearly explained, ideally when you sum up at the end.

It is important to close at the pre-announced time, as some people will need to get away. Others will be more than happy to stay around and talk further about the issues that have been raised. I often close a meeting by asking people for their help: 'We do not do this sort of thing all the time – indeed most of us are very inexperienced at it. So I wonder if you would be so kind as to help us by taking this card and pencil, and telling us three things: your name, what you thought of the event, and whether you would like to be invited to an Alpha course [or equivalent] which will be starting after this week is over.' At which point your colleague hands out either plain cards or the response card which the mission is using. Not everyone will comply, but most people will fill in one of these cards: after all, it is common in professional life. It may give an important insight into where they stand and suggest a stepping stone for the future.

It is not always easy to 'read' people from the comments they make in the discussion. I vividly recall a home meeting for gardeners. We walked around the garden having horticultural talk. Then we came in for a drink and the talk and discussion. The man who was most truculent and awkward took the proffered card and signed up for an Alpha course, to our utter amazement.

Personally invite all those present to another meeting in the mission programme, and then circulate. You may well have noticed that someone in the group has been visibly touched by what has been said. Go straight to such a person. But try to ensure that a team member has a word with everyone before they go; you will need to take the initiative in approaching people. I also often leave booklets on Christian commitment available near the door, and many of them disappear.

After the guests have gone, spend some time debriefing with the hosts, who will usually be thrilled, and feel able to talk further to their friends as a result of the evening. Ask them how they think it went, and learn from the experience. Pray with them. Encourage them to follow through with the guests. Take the cards back with you and hand them in to the leader at the next team meeting. The cards can then find their way to the follow-up co-ordinator.

These home meetings are enormous fun and often very profitable for opening up the whole topic of the gospel in a relaxed way with folk who would never otherwise talk about it. The more you enjoy it the better you will be at it!

Telling your story

An essential ingredient in a mission is the willingness of all team members to bear cheerful testimony to what Christ has done in their lives. It is arresting and, if done with genuine openness and enthusiasm, attractive. It may happen in the course of ordinary conversation, and then needs to be completely natural. It may take place in a home meeting. Or it may be an adjunct to a main talk in a larger meeting at the invitation of the preacher. Let us glance at these three contexts in turn.

When you give your testimony in the course of normal conversation, it starts from some suitable opening which presents itself. And the Christian speaks not about church or about religion but about Jesus. It is not difficult to do. 'May I share with you the greatest thing I have ever discovered?' The answer will invariably be 'Yes'. Then you can continue, 'It is the fact that Jesus Christ is alive and it is possible to know him.' That is likely to lead to an interesting conversation!

A slightly more formal testimony comes in the course of a home meeting. Remember that a testimony is not about yourself, and not about the past. It is about Jesus and the difference he makes to life here and now. In the New Testament 'witness' always means witness to Jesus, and we should keep it like that. Such witness is, of course, very valuable. It intrigues people, because it is unexpected. It is very natural too: when we have found treasure it is natural to want to share it. It is simple: anyone can do it. It usually opens up conversation. It has the advantage of bringing Christianity out of the expected area, the church, and into the arena of personal life. And best of all, it is unanswerable. Nobody can deny your experience, even if they have not had it for themselves. So it is a powerful weapon, not least in a home group situation where people can question you further about it, and others are often prompted to say something about their own experience.

When telling something of your story in a home meeting, keep it succinct and select those parts of the story with which it is easiest for your hearers to identify. It is worth throwing in the important fact that no two people come to Christ in precisely the same way, lest your hearers feel, 'Well, it was not like that in my case.'

When you are asked to give your testimony in a larger meeting, the situation is rather different. You are no longer the centre of attention, as you would be in a home meeting. Your role is to bring living personal illustration to some point the preacher is making. It is often best not to do this freestanding, before the main speaker comes on, but to be interviewed by the speaker at the appropriate time in the address. You and the speaker will spend some time beforehand, so that you understand what he or she wants you to concentrate on. Be clear how much time you have, and stick to it. Plan where you will stand and whether or not you will need to use a microphone. If so, practise with it beforehand, as much microphone work by inexperienced speakers is inaudible! And have a general idea of when in the course of the address you will be called on. Attention to details like these avoids delay and confusion in the meeting itself.

A few suggestions may help. Be prayerful, and ask the Lord to guide you as you speak. You will find you often say something entirely different from what you had planned, and that may be no bad thing! Centre your remarks on the person of Jesus and the difference he makes. Be selective, omitting irrelevant detail. Be warm and natural – a joke or a smile goes a long way. Total honesty is vital: never claim that faith in Christ has done more for you than it has. Be bold, with charm! Try to avoid any Christian jargon, or giving the impression that the Christian life is easy. Do not use notes. After all, it is your story, and you should know it! You are not there to preach. It is not 'You should' but 'I have found'. Keep it that way.

Remember that testimony is essentially spontaneous. Be watchful for opportunities to change the subject in conversation and move into spiritual things. We are called to 'redeem the time', and that means snapping up the opportunities that come our way. I long to see the Christians of this country come alive to the possibilities and the power of testimony. Most of our compatriots have no idea about real Christianity and that Jesus can be known personally. Testimony is likely to stop them in their tracks and make them wonder. And if we keep in mind a simple plan to say something first of our life *before* we came to Christ, then *how* and *why* we did so, and finally the *difference* he has made, it will give direction to our story and save us from the cardinal mistake of waffling.

For further material on training the team we turn to the next chapter.

13

The Team – How can we train them? Part 2

We have already seen some of the important areas to clarify with the mission team. We have several more to examine in this chapter.

Helping others to faith

The main aim of a mission is to bring people in repentance and faith to Jesus Christ, and make him the Lord of their lives. Accordingly it is essential that all members of the mission team are able to help an enquirer to that point.

It is not so often these days that people make an immediate response to the preaching of the gospel. Statisticians argue that folk usually need to hear the good news of Christ about ten times and presented in a variety of ways before they feel able to commit themselves. There may be several reasons for this. People are sceptical of any forceful presentation, be it from politicians, salesmen or preachers. There is a widespread commitment-anxiety in our society, whether for marriage or faith. And the gap between church and community has widened so greatly that most people would be quite unable to make an immediate act of commitment to the Christ of whom they know practically nothing. So most of the personal challenge to individuals by team members will generally be to sign up for an Alpha (or equivalent) course following the mission. This gives people an extended opportunity to look into the Christian faith and decide whether they will take it on board or not. And when people do undertake such a course, there is every possibility that as they look into the gospel they will come to a point of commitment, and it will be all the firmer because they understand what they are doing, and also because others on the course are pursuing the same quest.

However, that is not the whole story. In every mission there will be those who have reached the point where they need to act at once. Some of them may have been considering the Christian way for some years, on and off: they need to decide. Others may be untaught church-people who make church a regular part of their lives but have never realised they need to commit themselves to the one who has committed himself to us. We may well meet those caught up in the occult who need to make a decisive change of allegiance. And there are many other situations which lend themselves to a definite time of decision in a mission context. The team members need to be able to make the most of such opportunities.

Generally team members will find themselves talking about commitment after an effective address. As we have seen in an earlier chapter, there are ways of starting conversations and asking sensitive but direct questions which will reveal the kind of help needed by the individual. As you talk about the gospel with that person, it is helpful to have a rough outline in your head of the points you wish to cover. For example:

Repent . . . not just for the wrong things done, but for the underlying attitude of independence from God. Postmodern people are not impressed by accusations of wrongdoing, but are much more willing to recognise fragmented relationships, and this can be applied to us and God.

Realise . . . what God has done for you through Christmas, Easter and Pentecost. (You will need to unpack this, of course!)

Respond . . . not just to the message but to the Lord himself, welcoming his Spirit into heart and life.

Alternatively one could make use of four steps to faith, as basic as ABCD. In order to get right with God there is something to:

Admit . . . our failure to love him and give him access to our lives.

Believe . . . that our failures have not alienated him. He came to find us and longs to welcome us.

Consider . . . the cost of discipleship, which is never easy.

Do . . . While salvation cannot be earned, it must be received. We have to say 'Yes' to the Lord who has said 'Yes' to us.

Helpful Scripture verses might include the following. On human need: Romans 3:23, 6:23, 1 John 1:5, Isaiah 59:1f, John 8:34, together with the implications of Matthew 22:37–39 and James 2:10. On what God has done for us: Matthew 1:21, Romans 5:8, 1 Peter 2:24, 3:18, Isaiah 53:6, 1 Peter 1:3 and 5, Philippians 4:13. On the cost of discipleship: Matthew 6:24, Galatians 2:20, Romans 10:9–10. On the step of faith: John 3:16, 1:12, Revelation 3:20.

Of course, your friend may not be ready to respond positively. He may well say 'No' or 'Not yet'. If so, he will probably be weak on one of the three Rs we looked at above. Perhaps it is 'No' to *repentance*. Maybe he is convinced by the old English heresy that he has a heart of gold (Jeremiah 19:9 is potent here!) or that he has never done anyone any harm (take him through the Ten Commandments in Exodus 20. He will probably find he has broken them all in intention or act!). He may just feel he is fine as he is (but see Luke 13:3, Matthew 7:21–27 and Romans 3:10–20). These days it seems that the deepest repentance and return often comes through the story of the Prodigal Son. He is a profoundly postmodern figure. And his return to relationship speaks deep into the postmodern heart. At all events, it is certain that commitment without genuine repentance (and remember it is 'repentance towards God', not just for petty sins – Acts 20:21) soon melts away.

Perhaps it is that your contact has no *realisation* of what the Lord has done for him. Maybe he wonders how Christ's death so long ago can help him. Show that the infinite offering of Jesus more than covers all the finite people who ever have lived or ever will (Hebrews 10:11–14). Maybe he still thinks he can earn acceptance with God (but see Ephesians 2:8–9), or is somehow a Christian by dint of churchgoing without commitment (Romans 2:28–29 is relevant).

Or maybe his 'No' is in the area of *response*. Perhaps he confuses it with intellectual assent (but see James 2:19), or emotional experience: 'I tried it before, but it did not work!' You will need to do a bit of sensitive analysis at this point. But such claims usually suggest that the person has not begun true Christian living. Remember that the will is the hardest place to reach, and gently concentrate on that. I sometimes say to a person hovering on the brink of commitment, 'Right, you don't feel ready yet. What do you think is standing in your way? If we can sort that out to your satisfaction, will you turn to Christ?' Or 'I can see you need more time to think over this important decision. But can I ask you to commit yourself at least to coming to the Alpha course that will follow this week? It will give you an excellent chance to think things through.'

Unless there is extended time to talk, this will probably be the most natural solution. But it is a tremendous joy when you have the privilege of going further and helping the enquirer to faith – as suggested above.

Open air work

Sometimes a mission will embrace work in the open air. Of course Jesus and his followers did a lot of it, but it is rare in this country – perhaps because of our climate and partly because Christians remember with distaste the earnest preacher at the street corner from whom everyone shies away. But there is much to be said for it. We need to get out of the captivity of our church buildings and find ways to present the gospel attractively to those who may never go near a church.

There are two different groups of people in an open air presentation. One is the 'up-front' people, the dramatists, speakers, musicians, who need to remain free from conversation while the programme is going on. And there is 'the crowd', i.e. the rest of the team members, who will gather round the performers and watch, and engage in conversation some of those who stop and watch. Contrary to what you might imagine, 'the crowd' is more important than the 'up-front' people.

When planning an open air event, you may need to get permission from local authorities, and you must select a time and place where people naturally flow past in considerable numbers. The team will have met beforehand to pray and to collect a few response cards and booklets. The dramatists and musicians will have planned a programme for the presentation (usually about 20 minutes) so that all the material follows a logical sequence, presenting different aspects of the gospel. The compere will link the sketches, and interview members of the team about their Christian lives. The idea is to present an attractive and fast moving programme that will intrigue and hold a crowd.

Meanwhile the 'crowd' members of the team turn to a stranger standing near them and enquire, 'What did you make of all that?' Often a good conversation results. Some will be reluctant or maybe even hostile, but many will accept mission literature and you are likely to see some of them at an evening meeting if they have nothing else on – a direct result of the open air presentation.

Team members will probably not be accustomed to speaking to complete strangers, but this is a fast way to learn, and it is valuable training to engage in this sort of outreach. It can be hilarious, terrifying and hugely enjoyable!

Giving an evangelistic talk

The majority of your team will probably be inexperienced speakers and may find themselves thrown into an unaccustomed and rather frightening role of preaching or speaking in a significant mission event. I have devoted a previous chapter to this, for the benefit of those who may give major presentations during the mission. However, any member of the team may be called on to speak evangelistically in a home meeting, a youth event, a school, or a church service.

It is important to find out what sort of event it is. Are they churchgoers or not? Is it a large or small meeting? How do you fit in with the rest of the team, especially if others are reading, singing or acting? You need to be clear about your aim. Ask yourself what the talk is intended to achieve and keep aiming for it as you prepare. If you are not clear about your aim, nobody else will be. It must be simple and you must be able to express it in a single sentence.

Never underestimate the difficulty of speaking the good news of the gospel into today's selfish and pleasure-crazed society, eaten up by materialism, ignorant of the Bible and hooked on TV. Preaching itself is at a low ebb. There is often little sense of authority in the pulpit, little biblical content, little clear structure, little attractiveness in the message, little prayer for the whole venture. These are dangers to avoid.

In preparation, be open to God. Offer yourself wholly to him. Ask him to rekindle that first love of yours. Soak yourself in Scripture, and determine to present it without apology, so that it lives for your hearers. It is through the Word of God that people are born again. Let it be a sword in your hand!

Then it is vital to show yourself to be contemporary in your outlook, aware of the issues of the day. Concentrate on areas where people are vulnerable – lack of purpose and meaning in many lives, lack of love, hunger for fulfilment, loneliness and fear. And be Christ-centred in all you say. He is the person whom your hearers need to meet.

More specifically, here are a number of simple questions that will help the inexperienced speaker to prepare.

Whom am I addressing? This will affect my style, my language, how long I go on for, and even how I dress!

What do I want this talk to achieve? The aim is not the same as the subject matter. For instance, I might aim to encourage generous giving, but there are many passages I could use for that purpose. My aim must be crystal clear. Failure here is the most common mistake of many speakers.

What scripture do I want to use? It is an important choice which will, of course, affect the whole presentation.

How can I go about it? I suggest you mull over the chosen passage in your own devotional reading for several days, and make jottings in any order. It could be a number of verses, or a single verse, a theme or a Bible character. Then get a clear structure, with two or three main headings, and a good illustration from ordinary life to bring each one home. Avoid religious language (like 'salvation' and 'conversion') and take particular care with the way you intend to start and end. It is worth writing down the start and conclusion, but try not to write the whole thing out as it will spoil your spontaneity. Use headings instead, and put them on a piece of card that will fit neatly into your Bible without overlapping. In this way your notes will never be obtrusive.

How can I deliver it confidently? Confidence comes from careful preparation, from profound prayer, and from a sense of privilege at being Christ's ambassador on this occasion. My ease of manner makes such a difference to the hearers, especially if I smile, and look at them rather than have my head buried in my notes.

How do I want them to respond? It may be appropriate for you to suggest that they come and see you to join an Alpha course, or even to have a prayer of commitment at the end of your talk. You could suggest some such prayer as this: 'Lord, I am sorry to have kept away from you for so long. I am grateful that you came to find me and to die for me. Please come and share my life from this day onwards. Amen.' Something like that may seem so small and insignificant, and yet it can verbalise the desires in the heart of one or more of your hearers – desires that you can only guess at. Preaching is a wonderful mystery. You speak the good news as clearly as you can and you leave the outcome to God. Sometimes you will see clear results. At other times you will not. But be encouraged. As St Paul put it, 'Your labour is not in vain in the Lord.'

It is important to gather any responses that may be visible. You could ask people to come and see you if they would like to join a group or if they have prayed the prayer you suggested. You could urge undecided people to read a gospel with an open mind. You could also draw people's attention to appropriate material on the book table. And when it is all over, ask a close friend for honest criticisms and suggestions as to how you can improve as a speaker.

Those would be my five top priorities in training a team: telling one's story, helping someone to faith, giving a talk, leading a home meeting and street evangelism. But before ending this chapter I would like to add a note on two more areas that could well be covered.

Visiting

There are times when visiting can be quite a significant part of a mission. This may be when preparation has been poor and there are not enough events to keep the team busy; it may be an attempt to reach a hitherto untouched area or even a part of town where visiting is known to be welcome and fruitful. It can be of two kinds: cold-calling, or visiting people with whom the churches have had some contact, in which case lists need to be supplied by the ministers.

Visiting people's homes has the obvious value of showing the concern of the churches for the people living in their area. It gets Christians out of their buildings and onto the streets. And it has ample precedent in Christian history and in the example and teaching of Jesus himself. Where would Saul of Tarsus have been had not Ananias made that fateful visit to him – which he was most unwilling to undertake?

When visiting in a mission it is good to get clear about the geography, and if possible to have had a look at the local electoral roll so as to know the names of the occupants. Go equipped with a New Testament, pen, notebook (to take down details) and information about the mission. Have a good grasp in your mind of what goes on in the local churches for all age groups, so as to be able to recommend something appropriate.

It is often useful to go out two by two: there is a good precedent. Pray for each home you visit, as you knock on the door. Be friendly at all costs – they get plenty of troublesome visits. When the door opens, smile and introduce yourself, tell them you come from the church or the mission and say why you have come. Actually, you will have several aims. You will want to establish some sort of relationship which will enable local Christians to visit that home in the future. You will want to get information about the family and pass it on to the local church. You will want to tell them a bit about the mission, invite them to it, and leave a leaflet with them. This often opens up an opportunity to say something about Jesus, who alone can meet their need. It is, after all, this Jesus whom you are seeking to serve by coming on the mission. You will want to have a good idea of the regular organisations in the local churches, and try to connect one member of the family with one of them. You will want to see if there is some personal need in the home that the church could meet.

Of course there will be questions and objections. Sometimes they will be excuses: 'I went to church too much when I was young' . . . 'The minister has never called' . . . or 'I can worship God in my garden.' Sometimes they will be real difficulties, such as the divided state of the church, the multitude of religions, the implausibility of the church in a secular age, the problem of suffering, or the aching heart of a battered wife or a single mother. As we have seen in an earlier chapter it is helpful to try to analyse whether it is an excuse or a real difficulty and deal with it appropriately. Excuses come from hard hearts, difficulties from confused minds.

If you get a chance, you will want to pray for the house before you leave it. Prayer may not have been offered there for years, and yet people rarely refuse a suggestion that someone should pray for them if the offer is made humbly and warmly. Visiting is often disappointing, but you will hopefully have left something of the fragrance of Christ behind you, and every now and again you will come across a person whom God has clearly prepared to meet you – and that is tremendous joy. It makes the whole enterprise worthwhile.

Using Scripture

Finally, a word about using Scripture. Your team will believe that it is God's Word, and yet they may well be very coy about opening up a New Testament in a visit, or after a sermon. They hate being thought a Bible pusher. The answer to that is easy. It is the most natural thing in the world to say as some topic emerges in conversation, 'Why don't we take a look at what Jesus [or the New Testament] has to say on this interesting point?' Nobody can blame you for going back to the primary sources. And if they say they do not believe it, you can say, 'I am not asking you to believe it: just to discover what it has to say.' We read that 'the Word of God is living and powerful and sharper than a two-edged sword' (Hebrews 4:2), and it is important to expose people to its power. Time and again I have seen it overturn arguments and speak to the heart of the person I am with, when my words have failed to touch them.

When looking at a verse of Scripture with someone, I generally ask them to read it and then ask what it said to them. Other gentle questions and explanations may follow as we chat and I quietly pray that the Holy Spirit will apply the scripture to our friend. I try to avoid any suspicion of dullness, or Christian jargon like 'evangelism' or 'born again'. I want them to sense its power and truth. I want them to see that it is a book that knows us and speaks to our condition.

If we are to have any success as a mission team, we need training in all these different areas, and the value of them far outlasts any mission.

The Evaluation

14

Continuous Mission – Is it possible?

Evangelistic missions, such as we have been considering in this book, seem to me to have the effect of oxygen in the water. I speak as a would-be fly fisherman. And I think of a hot British August. All the fish tend to haunt the bottom of the pool: they are turgid and uninterested in anything I offer them. But when the first rains of September come, and the water is more turbulent, it is an entirely different story. The fish are revitalised by the fresh oxygen that has been injected into the water. The possibilities are now much greater – even for me!

The effect of a well-run and fruitful evangelistic mission is rather similar. A church may have been going along peacefully in its well-cultivated ruts, and then comes a mission. Outreach comes to the fore in the congregation's thinking. All sorts of church members get involved. Risks are taken. Those who had never gone public at work about their Christian commitment now come out of the closet and invite some of their colleagues to an event. People with artistic, secretarial, publicity and hospitality gifts find the church avid to use those gifts in the mission. There is a new vitality in the life of that church, quite apart from the arrival of new members, gained through the mission.

But can this new congregational liveliness be maintained, or is it doomed to die down again to its original state? Can mission be continuous? 'Continuous mission?' I hear someone saying. 'No fear! One mission has been bad enough, with all the extra work involved, and the unaccustomed activism. The idea of continuous mission is an abomination!'

I can sympathise with that point of view. Organising, preparing for, and executing a week-long mission is very demanding. The thought of doing something of the sort all the time is intolerable. Exhaustion would inevitably result, and instead of stimulating the vitality of the congregation, it would drain it. Obviously it is not possible to put on continuously the sort of intensive outreach which takes place in a mission. That is not what I would envisage by continuous mission. But let us look at it another way.

What if having an evangelistic mission every six or ten years is not necessarily the best way of carrying out the Great Commission? We normally think that it is the most lively churches which put on a mission like this every so often. But what if the occasional mission is the mark not of a healthy church, but of an unhealthy one? What if we should find that there are considerable disadvantages in one-off missions like this which need to be taken into account? Unless we have our eyes open to the dangers as well as the advantages of such a mission, we shall not be well placed to evaluate it.

The disadvantages of an evangelistic mission

We have considered the advantages of a one-off mission

in a previous chapter. But there are also a good many disadvantages to take into consideration. In the first place, not everybody in the local congregation will have got involved. There are sure to be some, perhaps a good many, who never wanted a mission in the first place, and determined to play no active part in it, but to keep their heads down until it was all over and then come up for air. And not just for air! They will complain about the money spent, the visiting team that came, the missioner himself and so on. They will spread the desire for a quiet life after all that activity, and will question whether anything was achieved by it all, thus spreading disillusionment.

Moreover, it is impossible during an intensive week of outreach to cover the whole range of a local congregation's responsibilities. The area of social concern, for example, can hardly be touched in so short a time. Patient and regular involvement is indispensable. As a result those whose main concern and gifts lie in meeting the social needs around them will not be particularly interested in the verbal proclamation which necessarily accompanies a mission. They may regard it as lop-sided, shallow and short-term.

Anyone who has looked into the variety of personality types revealed by Myers-Briggs will readily agree that there are many people who are likely to be thoroughly put off by the direct approach of an evangelist. Of course there are those who have a preference for 'judgement' (the Js), who are generally good at making decisions and sticking to them. These respond well to clearly laid out evidence warranting a decision. But there are many Ps, the people who prefer 'perception' and are by nature inquisitive. They like to keep open minds, and tend to revisit decisions in the light of new information. It is obvious that they are much less likely to be helped by the direct, challenging approach to be found in most missions. This is only one of the personality differences that can be found in all congregations. Inevitably, therefore, a mission is not going to appeal to everyone.

A mission is also a blunt instrument. It is hardly likely to have the sensitivity that good pastoral care over a period of time could show. There is inevitably an important emphasis on decision during a mission, and many are not ready to make it – at all events not in the form in which it is presented. A mission tends to call for black and white answers to rainbow-coloured questions!

Then there is always the possibility that the mission may be a fiasco. Perhaps the wrong missioner has been chosen for that particular university or congregation. Perhaps the team has made a lot of tactless mistakes. Perhaps the congregation has failed to enthuse over home meetings, and as a result the team has not had enough to do, and its members are seen as intruders. Perhaps the approach and preaching has been ill-suited to the local needs and concerns. There are all manner of possibilities on the road to disaster. In that case the very name of mission goes down in the collective memory of the congregation with the label 'to be avoided at all costs in future'.

But the most serious disservice a one-off mission can render is to usurp the ongoing challenge of the Great Commission. People can feel that they have done their bit by backing a mission once a decade, and they can congratulate themselves on some new people joining the church or Christian Union. They may feel that this exhausts their evangelistic calling as a church. Consequently the cutting edge of Christ's call to outreach is seriously blunted. Mission can be conveniently sidestepped as a general way of life for all churchpeople; after all we get involved in it every now and again – through a team that comes in and does it for us!

For all these reasons, over-reliance on a mission led by visitors can prove a hindrance rather than a help. The only justification for it is if it stimulates the local church to reach out to its neighbours appropriately with the gospel of Christ, and if it opens up some imaginative and suggestive ways of achieving this end. A mission must be a stimulus for ongoing evangelism, not a substitute.

Continuous mission

If this is so, we are driven back to some of the principles we considered at the outset. There is little point in taking a mission in a parish or student group that does not believe in conversion and accordingly has little interest in evangelism. There is little to be said for a mission that struggles all the time against the lethargy of the local church. Much of the point is to share in mission together and to encourage local participation – indeed to use methods (like home meetings) which can easily be reproduced locally long after the team has departed. I have increasingly come to realise that there is not a lot to be gained by having a team entirely composed of visitors who descend on the locality. It is much better if local Christians with a heart for mission can take the week off work and become full members of the team, alongside the visitors. In this way some people with considerable practical skills in evangelism are left in the church when the team departs.

It strikes me that the best model for an effective one-off mission is quite analogous to what happened to me recently. My three-year-old grandson was struggling with his scooter along some unmade road, and asked for a push. I said, 'OK. You have got to stay on the scooter and you are responsible for steering, but I will give you a good push, and we will go along together!' It worked well. A mission is only valuable if it incites and enables local participation, and does so in a way that facilitates replication. It gives the push to the scooter that is already moving. There is, for example, no point in having a couple of outstanding youth workers on a team if, when they leave, there is nobody in the local scene who can carry on the work, even if somewhat less brilliantly.

Then, how is it possible to 'maintain the spiritual glow', as St Paul expressed it? How can the momentum gained from a mission be maintained in the regular life of a church?

This is a question which has concerned me a good deal during my life. On the one hand, I have led a great many evangelistic missions, and on the other for twelve years I was Rector of a large church where continuous mission did take place. I know that it is possible to combine the two. But how? The following modest suggestions come from a good deal of practical experience.

The heart of the pastor

It seems to be the case that you cannot move a congregation much in any direction unless the pastor is keen on it. This shows what an awesome responsibility Christian leadership is, because it can quench initiatives as well as encourage them. But unless the pastor's heart blazes with a passion to reach people who are lost apart from Christ, evangelism is unlikely to figure largely in the programme of the church. Evangelism does not have to be his gift, but it *does* have to be his passion. He may well find others in the congregation who can do it much better than he, in which case his job is to build them up in every way he can, and give them plenty of opportunities to use their gift.

In this, as in so much else, example is crucial. If the congregation see that their pastor spends time among non-Christians with the aim of helping them towards faith, they will become motivated to influence their own friends towards the gospel. If the pastor is prepared to speak in homes to small groups about Jesus, before long he is likely to get more invitations from the congregation to do something similar in their home than he can handle. If the pastor is seen to put himself out for some new arrival in church, the idea becomes infectious in the church and the whole sense of hospitality and welcome (which lies at the heart of evangelism) expands. In a nutshell, the pastor has a key role in promoting outreach, and his example is critical.

The teaching ministry

The teaching ministry of the church can do an enormous amount to encourage and sustain enthusiasm for mission. Preaching is one obvious way. Preaching about the sheer grace of God until people feel it in their bones; preaching about the need of those without Christ; preaching about every member's responsibility to be a witness to Christ by life and lip. Preaching, too, about the vital importance of prayer for our non-Christian friends, for we cannot expect God to act without prayer.

Teaching extends far wider than preaching, of course. To have a number of adult baptisms in the congregation, whether in the church building or, better, in the local river or swimming baths, has an enormous impact. I was at a service recently when six adults were baptised outside the church building and then we went in for the remainder of the service. I found it very easy to preach relevantly on the whole need for outreach and conversion: people had seen it dramatised before their very eyes. That is why it is

a real help to the congregation to allow an opportunity
for new converts to say how they have found Christ. It
challenges those who are not there yet, and it teaches the
congregation the need to witness, without the pastor
having to say anything.

Another form of teaching which I found invaluable
was an annual training course. We originally hand-picked
30 members of the church for this ten-week course, but
thereafter there was no shortage of people applying for a
place on it. It was a lay training course, involving
worship, Bible study, teaching from the front, seminars,
and practical outreach. It lasted from 6.00 to 9.00 pm,
began with 20 minutes of worship led by lay people on
the course, and was followed by the main teaching of the
night, with overhead projection and notes. A wide variety
of topics was covered during those weeks, such as every-
member ministry, the heart of the gospel, Christian
service, giving a talk, leadership and helping someone to
faith. A break for refreshments was then followed by
small seminar groups round a leader, either handling a
new topic or deepening the general teaching just given.
Personal interviews between the group leader and
members of the group were important, as was the
outreach event the group planned either in our church or
in another church which requested it. This had a great
impact in discipling the key people in the church, who in
turn realised how they could help others. And as this
continued year by year many in the church were built up
into effective Christian workers, able to give a short talk,
able to lead someone to Christ, and keen to use their
God-given gifts in his service.

Preaching for decision

One of the very obvious ways of keeping outreach and

confidence in the whole evangelism enterprise alive is for the pastor to hold an invitation service from time to time in the course of the year. Not too often, but not too rarely either. Four times a year might be a good idea. It will have been carefully prepared. There will be extended prayer times for friends whom members of the congregation hope to bring. There will be careful plans made for the actual service. All sorts of apparently small things make a lot of difference. It is important to have a couple of your most gracious Christians on welcoming duty, and to make the whole service deliberately visitor-friendly (but not so different from usual that it shocks them if they come back next week!). The music needs to be carefully prepared with the non-churchgoer in mind – what would help such a person most? A couple of testimonies would be valuable: one on the value of a nurture course by someone who has recently attended, and one by someone who has fairly recently come to faith. This all builds up expectancy in newcomers: this church runs courses for unchurched people like them, and this faith makes a difference to ordinary people, does it? This will make them predisposed to listen carefully to the address.

Great care will of course be lavished on the preparation of this talk. It needs to be arresting from the very first words, warm, Christ-centred, and challenging. It is probably best these days to challenge unchurched people to start exploring the faith, rather than attempt to win them to Christ then and there.

You will have leaders for a new nurture group ready for such people, and you will want to start it the very next week so as to avoid people slipping away. Alternatively you may prefer to use the nationally recognised Alpha or Emmaus or Christianity Explained courses. All of these can profitably be used to help newcomers come to faith and get established in it.

It amazes me when I find churches that never have a challenge to commitment in their sermons, or are so tied to the liturgical year that they never depart from speaking about the Epistle and Gospel of the day, whatever the needs of the congregation may be! Having said that, of course, Easter and Christmas and carol services are the three most obvious occasions when an evangelistic address is entirely appropriate liturgically, and when the maximum number of non-regulars may be seen in church. It is madness to miss such opportunities. I know many churches which do not preach at their carol service, and as a result the congregation slips away feeling warmed, maybe, but as untaught and unchallenged as when they came in. God uses preaching to change lives. The wise pastor knows this, and will from time to time preach for decision, and then carefully nourish those who sign up for a nurture course. This will naturally do much to encourage ongoing evangelism and godly expectancy in the congregation. It will also involve some of the lay leaders in helping to run that course and as they see new believers coming to life, that in itself will spread the evangelistic zeal in the church.

But the pastor should not rely exclusively on set-piece evangelistic sermons. Many other opportunities will arise within and beyond the church building to do some gentle evangelism. I think of weddings, funerals, and services for business-people, scouts and guides. The opportunities are legion, if we have the heart to take advantage of them.

The Alpha course

Alpha is now big business. It is a Christian induction course skilfully designed for the postmodern market, based round food, laughter, questions about the meaning of life, unashamed Bible teaching on the major topics in Christian belief and behaviour, companionship with others on the same journey, and the possibility of gaining hands-on spiritual experience through the Holy Spirit Day or Weekend. It has proved its worth in all sectors of society despite the fact that the superb video talks are very much upper middle class English productions. Somehow that does not seem to matter, and most people take to it like ducks to water. Countless parishes in England and more than a hundred other countries are finding this one of the most impressive means of outreach. It is non-threatening, informative and open-textured: no questions are regarded as out of court. It is not authoritative 'take-it-or-leave-it' stuff dished out by the clergy, but is usually lay led, encourages everyone to make their own exploration, and gives ample opportunity for personal encounter with the living God, and the enrichment of life this brings. In fact it fits the varied social situation in Western countries like a glove, and is quite effective as well in Africa and Asia. So I would recommend having an Alpha course going three times a year.

The first one or two times you run it in your church you will generally find that church members are the main takers. But after they have seen what an effective instrument it is for non-pressurised evangelism they will start asking their friends, and before long you have a self-perpetuating series of Alphas, as members who have been converted during one course cannot wait until they can get their friends to the next one. To be sure, there are weaknesses in the course. There is arguably too strong an emphasis on tongues, which St Paul valued but saw as a genuine but comparatively unimportant spiritual gift. There is little about the sacraments in the course. And it is quite possible to enjoy it all but emerge completely unchanged if there has not been any effective personal care by the leaders to help individual members clinch matters.

Sometimes you find clergy complaining that they have tried Alpha and it did not do any good. What you then discover is that they had economised on the need to provide a dinner, and substituted weak cups of tea instead! And for fear of having anything as dangerous as a day on the Holy Spirit, they skipped that part of the course. No wonder Alpha did not work. To omit two elements as crucial as the fellowship that develops round meals, and the decision to invite the Holy Spirit to come and invade your life, is sheer folly. No, you must do the whole course in full, if you want it to be effective. It will have the added benefit of involving many of the church in praying, in organising the room, in preparing and serving the food, in washing the dishes and in helping pastor the group. And because they are involved in something which is changing lives, inevitably the spiritual temperature remains high and the desire for evangelism remains keen.

Teams

One of the best ways of maintaining a high spiritual climate and love for evangelism in either student or church situations, is to take small teams out with you. If you are invited to give a talk one evening, take two or three people with you, and allow them a part in the enterprise. If you are asked to preach somewhere, take a couple of people and use them to testify during your sermon. If you are invited to take a weekend event, make it not a solo but a team event. If you are asked to do a mission in a parish, ask whether you may bring a team and also whether it would not be a good idea to involve other churches in the locality, preferably across the denominations.

Ministry using teams is one of the best forms of training and one of the most effective forms of outreach. I have used it for many years, in particular with teams of young people, mostly undergraduates in their early twenties. Each year we would train and then take such a team to a town where many churches had united to get involved in the project. Usually the team was 80–100 strong, with many of them very new Christians. But the impact of those missions was enormous, and it gave great confidence, strength and growing maturity to those who came on them. They danced a conga in the streets, they preached and sang and dramatised in the open air, they led meetings in homes, meetings for children and events for youth, they taught in schools, fed the hungry, and saw scores of people, most of them far their seniors, coming to trust Christ and join his church.

At other times of year the students of one or more of the Oxford colleges would invite me and a small team into the bar of their college where a very mixed reception awaited me (and/or shouted me down!). But these visits enabled people to hear something of the gospel who would never have darkened the door of a church, and several of them found Christ, to the delight of the courageous students who had invited us in.

This did not just happen in the past: it still continues in a variety of ways. A friend of mine has in recent months been discovering many new forms of outreach taking place in Britain today, largely unsung but none the less effective. One is a team of youngsters from a large Liverpool Kidz Club and their leaders, who set Bible verses to the tunes of TV ads and teach them, with their meaning, to some of the roughest and toughest kids in the city. The leaders have won the affection and trust of these children by dogged faithfulness and visiting them each week in their homes. Another team run a Christian café in the heart of York and are constantly lending a listening ear to and praying with the many people, often with deep needs, who drop in after visiting York Minster. Across town is Liz. She gave up her teacher training job and her secure middle-class life because she felt God calling her to work with people 'not of her class'. She and a little team have been working on a housing estate full of drugs and alcohol where nearly all have criminal records and broken lives. She tells how many responded to the healing love of Christ and just went and told others. More than 50 people came to faith in a year! In Newquay young 'Dawn Patrol' teams take the love of Christ to the summer surfers, and in Cumbria another team have taken over a large barn which they use for young people with nowhere to go. Ingredients? Skateboarding – and worship. And of course in Manchester a truly remarkable work is being done by Andy Hawthorne and The Message Tribe.

It is as well to realise that there is a quiet explosion of mission going on around Britain today. The media delight in spreading depressing news about the decline and imminent death of Christianity in the West and the absence of young people in our churches. But the church has often, throughout its long history, been told to lie down and die, and it keeps rising to new life! And young people may not be plentiful in Matins and Evensong, but you will find large numbers of them in teams like these, offering two or more years of their lives without pay to go anywhere and do anything for Christ with vast international teams like Youth With A Mission and Operation Mobilisation. It is the young people in particular who are currently forming teams to spread the gospel in a way appropriate to their culture. And anyone who wants to deepen the passion for mission in their church or university would do well to reflect on the impact of mission teams, even of inexperienced people, and mobilise such teams to further the continuous mission of the people of God. For mission is the forgotten dynamite in the church!

BOOKS *IN PRINT*
BY THE SAME AUTHOR

1500 Illustrations of Biblical Preaching (Baker)
Adventure of Faith (Zondervan)
After Alpha (Kingsway)
Asian Tigers for Christ (SPCK)
Baptism, its Purpose, Practice & Power (Hodder & Stoughton)
Bible Reading for Amateurs (Hodder & Stoughton)
But Don't All Religions Lead to God? (Sovereign)
The Church Without Walls (Paternoster)
Churchgoing for Amateurs (Hodder & Stoughton)
Critical Choices (IVP)
The Empty Cross of Jesus (Hodder & Stoughton)
Evangelism for Amateurs (Hodder & Stoughton)
Evangelism in the Early Church (Kingsway)
Evangelism Through the Local Church (Hodder & Stoughton)
I Believe in Satan's Downfall (Hodder & Stoughton)
The Message of Matthew (IVP)
Michael Green Omnibus (Hodder & Stoughton)
My God (Eagle)
Strange Intelligence (IVP)
Thirty Years that Changed the World (IVP)
You Must Be Joking (Hodder & Stoughton)

Evangelism in the Early Church

by Michael Green

'I cannot conceive how anyone could read this book without having his evangelistic vision renewed and zeal kindled.'

John Stott

Michael Green combines his undoubted talents both as evangelist and theologian as he focuses, with numerous quotes from the primary sources, on evangelism 'in the strict sense of proclaiming the Good News of salvation to men and women with a view to their conversion to Christ and incorporation into his Church.'

This is a comprehensive evaluation and reappraisal of the main aspects of evangelism in the early church, concentrating on the New Testament period but also providing a topical treatment of evangelism up to the middle of the third century.

This revised edition introduces the reader to the latest finds and developments in scholarship.

'A notable achievement.'   *Church Times*

'The indispensable basis for a consideration of modern evangelism.'

I. Howard Marshall

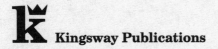 **Kingsway Publications**